The heyday Independent Officer in England and Wales. 1950's – 1970's

By

Geoff Kenure

Copyright © 2018 Geoff Kenure

ISBN: 978-0-244-71173-3

All rights reserved, including the right to reproduce this book, or portions thereof in any form. No part of this text may be reproduced, transmitted, downloaded, decompiled, reverse engineered, or stored, in any form or introduced into any information storage and retrieval system, in any form or by any means, whether electronic or mechanical without the express written permission of the author.

For Kathy

"Love bears all things, believes all things, hopes all things, endures all things"

First Corinthians 13:7

Contents

Introduction

Chapter 1	Interview?
Chapter 2	Advise, assist and befriend
Chapter 3	Officer of the Court or Court Officer
Chapter 4	Band of Brothers……and Sisters
Chapter 5	Learning the Ropes
Chapter 6	Social Casework
Chapter 7	Social Caseworker
Chapter 8	Transition
Chapter 9	Individual Case Management
Chapter 10	Practical Caseload Management
Chapter 11	Engaging in the Clients' milieu
Chapter 12	The Probation Court Report – to Enquire or to Inquire
Chapter 13	The Probation Order of the 1960's
Chapter 14	Breach of Probation Order
Chapter 15	Courts – A market place
Chapter 16	Home Visits
Chapter 17	Offenders and Mental Illness.
Chapter 18	Opinion.
Appendix 1	Case Study - Billy Hall
Appendix 2	Slips of the Report Writer's pen

Introduction

Heyday may be defied as – something's greatest period of success, popularity, activity, or vigour

*

This book uses the stories and experiences from my working life to attempt to shed light on what it was like to work in, arguably, the final heyday years for a probation officer working as a relatively independent professional.

It is my argument that probably the best time to work as an independent probation officer in England and Wales was in that period from the mid-1950s to the mid-1970s. It was, I would say, a period when the maximum responsibility for the work of supervising offenders lay with the individual officer, in a tripartite contract between court, offender and supervising probation officer. In that period the role of the organisation was to support the work of the front line independent officers with limited managerially imposed requirements. It was, in my contention, a heyday period, as increasingly after the mid-1970s managerialism took hold of the probation services of the day leading to an increasingly top down management, and an insidious de-professionalisation of the independent probation officer role.

In making this case of an independent professional, I will look at the service structure as well as my training, philosophy, values and practice as a serving probation officer from the mid-1960s up to a point in the late 1970s, by which later date the growth of managerialism had, in my contention, begun to significantly erode the independence of the professional probation officer role. That managerialism, as part of the move to centralised control of the probation service by the Home Office, developed in parallel with the radical revision of sentencing which led to the Criminal Justice Act 1991. When enacted in 1992, this Act brought to an end, after 85 years on the statute books, the Probation Order.

Upon recently clearing out my home, my old notes from my training to be a probation officer came out, *en route* to the recycle bin.

They arrived there; and two days later came out again.

Their resurrection was due to them sparking the thought that perhaps there was a story to be told about what it was like to be a probation officer in the 1960s and 1970s up until till the death of the "original" Probation Officer of England and Wales in 1992. This is not intended as a 'rosy view' of some 'good old days', a pastime in which older people, amongst whom I am now to be numbered, so often indulge. More it is an attempt to paint a picture of the role of an individual probation officer in the era to which I refer.

I will try not to make judgement upon any subsequent changes; rather, I will leave the reader to draw their own conclusion as to how the values and practices of those distant days square with the values and practices of later times.

In telling the story, I will attempt to provide some context as to the ethos of the probation service of the 1960s both as I was taught the values by those who preceded me and as I experienced it, together with what it was like to work in a relatively large city probation office of the day. I will look especially at the links between probation officers and the courts. But, I will also try to give a flavour of the work of the day by reference to various cases and experiences of my working life.

I began training as a probation officer in the 1960s and worked in that capacity until I retired in 2003. In the second half of my career I was a middle manager, a senior probation officer with responsibilities for training and the provision of probation services to local courts. All through the period I will be writing about, I supervised clients (offenders). Also, throughout the whole of my career, I was involved with the magistrates and judges in local courts and I treasure the plaque in my hallway which reflects the gratitude of the local Bench for my 34 years of service to my local courts. After retirement, I worked for myself for 12 years training people in court advocacy skills; focussing mainly on staff entering either the probation or youth offending services.

Of course this will be an idiosyncratic view of the period, and some who read this may have worked in those days and feel that my view differs from theirs. This would be unsurprising, since the probation services of the day differed from place to place because, as I will explain, they were managed and run locally with very general guidelines and light touch from centre.

I see no particular value in referring to the city involved, this is because, in my experience, people can make judgements about places, and I just want to reflect a more general view of the work of the probation officer in the period discussed. However, for those acquainted with it there will be no difficulty in its identification. I will also avoid identifying most people, but again some public figures will be known to many who knew the city. Former colleagues may recognise parts of themselves, but, I have tried to anonymise so far as I can. As to the offenders; I have tried to ensure that no third-party will be able to identify them, although if they remember me as their officer, they may also recognise themselves!

It is my intention to make this an interesting read, being openly personal about my experiences and attempting to capture the spirit of the times, and although, in parts, there is need to make reference to sources, I am not going to interrupt the narrative by quoting them. I just want to paint a picture of the job I started in the 1960's and to show how, in those days of relatively independent local justice, the probation officer held a very loosely regulated independent professional role. In short it is my contention that they were the heyday years for that role. Apart from the first and last chapter each will begin with an anecdote which will hopefully amplify the ethos of the times.

Chapter 1
Interview?

"Choose a job you love and you will never have to work a day in your life." Confucius

*

After three years training to be a probation officer I had nearly qualified and was looking for a job. As a single man who had survived on a grant from the Home Office to train, I could have chosen any part of the country. However, my choice was narrowed due to the inconvenient fact that I had fallen in love just at that time. My fiancée and I had met during training and she was seconded from her job and had to return to it for a minimum of three years as a condition of their paying for her attendance on the course. So, my hope was to get a post in one of the three probation services near her place of work, so that we could marry and set up home together. I wrote to all three services on the same day, a few months before the end of my training.

Even though it was before the two tier system of first and second class which did not begin till September 1968 the General Post Office of that day was on the ball for the following day I received a telephone call at my 'digs' from the principal probation officer of one of the city areas. City areas in the 1960s were usually significantly understaffed. He invited me to attend at their office the following week, "just come for a look round to see our setup" he had said. I was impressed by the speed of his response and agreed to attend.

During the morning I was shown round the office; a tatty converted warehouse. I met a number of officers and the general impression I had was a welcoming one. At the end of the morning the principal took me over to the City Hall, where the magistrates' courts were then housed, and after a short tour took me for lunch in the staff canteen on the top floor. Meat and two veg., followed by spotted dick and custard; quite a feast for an impoverished student. After lunch we went downstairs and he asked me to wait outside a door marked "Chairman of the Probation Committee".

After only a few minutes I was invited in. There sat a lady, behind a desk, which, as well as papers held a very fetching hat. It was customary in those days, in that city, for all women magistrates to wear a hat when sitting on the bench.

She gave me a broad smile and our conversation, blunt and to the point, went as follows:

"The principal officer tells me you are a nice young man"

"Errrr......well thank you madam."

"Now tell me when does your training course finish?"

"Well it goes on to the end of September madam" (it was then July)

"Oh dear! As long as that! Well, never mind, have the weekend off and start the first Monday in October"

Stutteringly I replied, "But I haven't applied for a job madam"

"You want to work don't you!!!!"

And, of course, I did.

I left somewhat bewildered, and within a couple of days I received in the post confirmation of my appointment, together with a job application form to complete………………..in the same envelope!

Chapter 2
Advise, assist and befriend

"It shall be the duty of probation officers to supervise the probationers and other persons placed under their supervision and to advise, assist and befriend them."
Home Office Probation Rules 1949.

*

"Follow me in and keep quiet" my guide said to me, as we entered the number one court of the Quarter Sessions. It was my first day as a qualified probation officer; only a confirmation year to go and I would be fully trained, and endorsed, in the job. We entered through the half glass doors and were in the body of the court. Ahead of me a passageway ran across the courtroom to a similar entrance on the other side. To my immediate right was the dock, a towering wall of wood about 9 feet high with a small black rail on top. This raised the prisoner above the well of the court and almost on eye level (but not quite) with the judge. To my immediate left were the tables for the barristers and their instructing solicitors, and beyond that a slightly raised dais for the court clerk, and above that the bench. We turned to our left and took the side benches two up from the courtroom floor.

We had arrived at the point where the defence barrister had just ended his mitigation in the case of a burglar who had already pleaded guilty. After a short silence the man in the wig on the bench, Mr Recorder ...... Whatever (memory gets less efficient as the length of time from my first pension cheque increases) called for the prisoner to rise and said, "It falls to me to sentence you for two counts of house burglary, which, to your credit, you have admitted here today". I felt most uncomfortable since Mr Recorder Whatever was looking directly at me. I was in turn, embarrassed, anxious and angry, since I had admitted no such thing. But, before I had time to formulate a response, my guide, a probation officer colleague who was showing me round, whispered "I find this Recorders squint disconcerting, his good eye is staring straight at the defendant but his other eye seems to be looking directly at us." I relaxed as the prisoner was led away to start his term of 18 months imprisonment.

As the next case was called I wondered whether the pathfinders in my chosen profession also experienced embarrassment, anxiety and anger as they started working in the courts in the years after 1907. They were embarking on the development of the work of supervising probation orders which was to experience some 85 years of life and to establish itself as a worthy profession in the eyes of the criminal justice system in England and Wales.

*

Two completely separate strands, I suggest, led to my early predecessors coming into existence. The first was the demand by the judiciary for a new sentence of the court to replace some of those that had passed their "sell by date" or were no longer appropriate. In the late 1800's the original suspended sentence (the one that involved a rope and a trapdoor) had been overused and was a bit extreme for some offences. Deportation had run its course (Australia already had sufficient for a good cricket team) and the fine was problematic as the debtor's jails were full and defendants could not offer one pound per week from their Social Security benefits - because there weren't any such benefits.

So courts, in different parts of the country, started to experiment to adapt the conditional discharge. It was, and still is, an exceptionally valuable sentence. It involves releasing the defendant without penalty for a period of up to 3 years with the condition that they should not re-offend in that specified period. Of course one of the main principles of sentencing is to prevent re-offending and this fits the bill to the tee. However, if the person re-offends in the allotted period then the court has the power, not only to deal with the person for the new offence, but also to resurrect the original offence and sentence them for that in addition.

There was one slight problem. Courts noticed that, however earnest the defendant might be in accepting the conditional discharge and assuring the court that they would comply there were three types of person who were doomed to fail. One type they could do nothing about was the person dedicated, for whatever reason, to follow a life of crime. The other two types with the potential to fail on the conditional discharge could actually have their potential for success raised. The first type was the person with a poor memory and / or who became complacent about the existence of the conditional discharge before it had run out. The second was the person with significant social difficulties, like homelessness or lack of income, encouraging them to turn to offending to meet their own, or their families, basic needs.

So these progressive 'sentencers' (a term I use to embrace both judges and magistrates) started to add additional informal conditions to the conditional discharge. Thus, for example, where an apprentice stood before the court, the employer, if willing, was asked to enter into some recognisance with the court that they would, in effect, monitor the offenders' behaviour to remind the person to keep out of trouble. Others, recruited to the role of reminding the offender of their responsibilities to the court, included local worthies such as ministers of religion. So now these courts had established a 'conscience figure' who would remind those offenders, subject of the conditional discharge, of the need for them to keep out of trouble. Thus the forgetfulness issue was addressed. Then for those with practical issues driving offending a helper may be chosen who could advise the offender how to address their specific problems.

The second precursor strand leading to the coming into existence of my predecessors, derived from the growth of charities in the final quarter of the 19th century. One hundred years before the advent of the welfare state, the state of welfare in England and Wales was pretty awful. If there was no work available to you, or you were unfit to work, and you had no family support, you were in trouble. As the country moved even further from an agrarian to an industrial society the greater became the problems. For those in need, charities began to spring up who would help people with a particular category of problem. One such was the Church of England Temperance Society. The type of clientele they worked with is evident from the name on the tin .....or should that be, bottle.

Their main aim was to get people 'on the wagon', but in the 1860's, they were sparked into further action by a letter from a Mr

Rainer, who drew their attention to his observation that 'something should be done to break the cycle of people appearing before the magistrates courts for drunkenness time and again.' Being a religious organisation they decided to create the London Police Courts Mission and to send "missionaries" out to the local Southwark Magistrates Courts to try to meet up with, and help those who had appeared for drunkenness and to counsel them towards a life of abstinence and sobriety.

These missionaries worked with magistrates to develop a system of releasing offenders on condition that they kept in touch with the missionary and accepted guidance. By 1880 there were 8 full time missionaries in place and the Mission had opened shelters providing vocational training and some residential accommodation. By 1886 the Probation of First Offenders Act allowed courts nationally to follow the metropolitan example; few did so. The police court missionaries no doubt helped many individuals, but for my purposes, the most important thing was that they gradually established a relationship of trust with the local courts. The courts could see them doing their work and they were both grateful and impressed.

It was shortly after the turn of the century that the two strands came together in the Probation of Offenders Act 1907. The idea, from a legal perspective, of the probation order was born in terms of combining the conditional discharge with mandatory added supervision. There would be formal requirements including the need to keep in touch with the probation officer in accordance with instructions which may from time to time be given, including receiving visits at their home. There would also be a requirement to inform the officer of any change of address. In certain circumstances an extra requirement "to secure the good conduct of the offender" could be added. Then, so as to be able to enforce these requirements, there was a provision that if the offender failed to observe any of them, the probation officer could initiate a complaint for "breach of the terms of the order". If a local justice could be satisfied that there was a *prime facie* case to answer, then a summons or warrant could be issued to bring the matter back before the relevant magistrates court, known as the "supervising court'. If the breach was proved to the satisfaction of the court then the offender could either be dealt with for the breach, effectively a slap on the wrist, with or without a minor added penalty, and an exhortation to buck their ideas up, with the order remaining in force. Alternatively, the offender could be dealt with for the original offence and the order would be consequently ended. Furthermore the order could be reviewed if the offender was convicted of another offence during its currency. As a result, we had the probation order starting in 1907 which was to continue to be an order of the court until its abolition for all new offences committed after April 1992, upon the implementation of the Criminal Justice Act 1991.

But, who would undertake the supervision of these "probationers" as they would come to be known? Well, since the courts would make the orders, and local justice independent of centre was very much the order of the day, it was decided that this responsibility of recruiting the probation officers would be handed to local magistrates' courts groups, or petty sessional areas. This happened over time but became mandatory in the Criminal Justice Act 1925. They were to receive funds from centre but they then were responsible for employing and overseeing the staff they appointed.

Now, in 1907, whom could the local courts think of that were likely to be trustworthy and reliable, and who may have some experience of the problems of offenders, and were even vaguely experienced in working with the sort of people who appeared in court? Well, what about those nice police court missionary people whom they had got to know over the preceding years?

And so it was that many of the people appointed as probation officers in the beginning had originally been police court missionaries. Thus, unsurprisingly, the ethos of the early probation officers in undertaking their work with offenders was based on the moral teachings of the Christian church. Secularism gradually grew, and when training started after the Second World War, social casework theory began to replace religious ideas. Yet in my office when I arrived there were practising Quakers, Methodists, Anglicans, a Catholic priest who had left that calling for the probation calling, and as one wag said, enough of one denomination to 'start a bloody Salvation Army band.'

Going back to the early probation officers, there were not too many requirements imposed by centre for the magistrates to consider in making appointments to their local probation service. One significant one was the requirement that each area had to have at least one man and one woman and the women officers only supervised female offenders. Given that in those days the number of females on probation was far less than the males, some of the female staff worked on a part-time basis. Nevertheless, it is an interesting development in women's equality, given that at the time women did not even have the vote. It established a place for female staff right from the very beginning, even though no doubt, in the mores of the day, it was most probably done for paternalistic and sexist reasons.

So, how would the newly appointed probation officer have felt as they took their place in a court for the first time? Probably, like me, they experienced the embarrassment of feeling self-conscious in a, new to them, formal setting where everyone else seemed totally at ease and self-confident; except maybe the defendant. Anxious that they would not do or say something that made them look or feel silly, but they may nevertheless have wished to have intervened in the occasional case but lacked the knowledge or skills to do so, until months or years later when they learned the ropes and had established their credentials.

But those early officers were developing a role which was to become a very independent one due to the structure, or rather lack of structure, of the fledgling organisation. Effectively there was little central control; centre mainly provided the funds and the local justices ran their own probation service. The justices were responsible for hiring and firing officers and for overseeing their work. But each officer was independent, making decisions about how to supervise the offender, and their accountability in each case was directly to the court.

With minor changes things progressed until that post Second World War period when many significant changes to the social structures of the country were made. For example, the Education Act 1944, the National Health Service Act 1946, the National Assistance 1948 and also that year a very significant Criminal Justice Act. In that Act it stated that "it shall be the duty of probation officers to supervise the probationers and other persons placed under their supervision and to advise assist and befriend them.... in accordance with any directions of the court". And so was enshrined in legislation the phrase which became the watchwords of all probation officers from thenceforward for over 20 years, and they were words which were significant for me in entering my new profession.

The Criminal Justice Act 1948 created Probation Areas which were to be coterminous with Metropolitan Police Court areas, and it set out the basis for probation orders for the next 25 years. It did also enshrine the requirement that the Home Office now had control over the training and confirmation in post of probation officers. But the hiring and firing (subject to ratification by the Home Office) was done by the justices, on the newly formed probation committees. These committees were drawn from members of the bench or benches in a petty sessional area elected to serve on this committee. In my experience they took a great deal of interest in the work of the officers and in the service as a whole. Again it was my experience in the 1960's that they retained a paternalistic view of "their officers".

Through the prescribed medium of Case Committees they were directly involved in the work of the service, by having officers periodically bring before them a selection of case files, and requiring them to explain, to the members of the committee, what they were doing and why. If the committee felt they were dissatisfied with the work they would say so and could order an officer to take a different course such as, for example, ordering the officer to bring a case back to court for breach, where the officer had decided to give a further chance before doing so.

So the structure set by the 1948 Act was to wrest some responsibility from local justices in relation to training and confirmation in post of new officers, but a lot of responsibility remained with the justices who, whilst they had an overall management role they did not manage on a day-to-day basis. The 1949 Probation Rules clarify the roles of the local services Principal Probation Officer; note the wording, not a chief but a principal, which to me implies not a director, more a first amongst equals. Also the senior probation officer had a role description which was, effectively, to support the officers for whom they were administratively responsible.

So, dear reader, you might say how do you argue that the individual officer was as independent as you imply? After all there were principal officers and senior officers prescribed in the rules. So here I must quote directly from the Probation Rules of 1949 in relation to senior officers. "They are to supervise and advise upon the work of probation officers working under them." It goes on to specifically prescribe that they should "allocate work between officers, examine and advise on the way records are kept and how their officers manage their working time".

Whilst one could argue the word 'supervise' has a directive implication that, in my view is modified by the following word "advise" which does not. Indeed to advise is to suggest a course of action which may, or may not, be followed by the person advised. In my experience of the time, most senior officers took the view that they were more advisers than supervisors and that, at the end of the day, the officer was accountable for the management of their cases ultimately to the court. I would pray in aid (that phrase comes to mind from too many years sitting courts listening to poor speeches of mitigation by defence solicitors) that the descriptions above about what senior officers should specifically do, is directed towards the practical time management issues not the case specific ones.

Thus, the ethos of the service I experienced upon entry was one where you, the officer, were responsible for the individuals placed in your care by order of the court. You had a responsibility to them but ultimately to the court. You felt that you worked for the local magistrates, and you met those magistrates who were on probation committees fairly regularly. Even with a bench of about 300 magistrates in my city, you also got to know at least the senior magistrates, the ones who chaired the benches, by dint of presenting your own court reports, appearing in court when one of your cases had re-offended or whilst being on court duty.

Once I got into things I felt that I had got a job where I had wide ranging individual professional responsibility and accountability.

In short, it felt to me that my role was that of an independent professional.

Chapter 3
Officer of the Court or Court Officer

'Officer' has been defined as a holder of a public, civil, or ecclesiastical office.

*

A few months after my initial court visit to the recorder with the squint, I was getting to grips with my new role. One of the jobs required of all officers, was that of being on a rota for court duty from time to time. By the time of this incident I was familiar with the duties I was required to undertake. These mainly consisted of taking reports and papers to court, getting results from those cases which involved fellow officers and generally answering any queries court may direct to the probation service. But little in the court duty work of those days could be described as proactive.

I had made the acquaintance of some of the court clerks (now more properly dubbed Legal Advisers) most of whom were helpful - though a few were not. I had made my number (old naval expression for a signal made by an approaching newcomer wanting to join a squadron or fleet) with the court ushers. These folk, often retired persons in those days, for the pay was poor, were key people to help you get information from the courts it was physically impossible to keep tabs on, because of the geography of the building and the fact that there was usually only one person to cover the five lesser courts. One colleague was permanently based in the main remand court.

My experience was sufficient to be aware of the leading magistrates of the day and I was aware that some had particular reputations for one foible or another. One senior magistrate of the day was Stanley. A man for whom a sentence including the words "gladly", "fools", "suffer", and "does not", comes readily to mind. Added to which, his temperament appeared to be volatile. I often thought that he would have fitted well into the Scottish legal system which held that wonderful legal sentencing disposal, not available to courts in England and Wales, namely, the penalty of an Admonishment. Stanley, I would offer, would be able to admonish with the very best of them.

Having introduced the players in this story I am about to tell, it is now crucial to describe the geography of the five courts I was scheduled to cover on that day. I have already referred earlier to the beautiful Victorian number one court, which on the day in question, was again being used by the Quarter Sessions and the magistrates courts had limited space and some were forced to use committee rooms in the City Hall, instead of all the usual courtrooms.

My courts to cover were situated in different parts of the building; two in one part and three more in another. I was then in my 30s and physically quite fit, yet to travel from one end of my realm of the day to the other, involved the descent of two flights of spiral steps, and the ascent of two long marble sets of stairs; or vice versa. In between the two parts of the building there was the need to descend below the number one court and ascend again the other side. My best time from one further point of my empire to the other would be between two and three minutes, if successfully able to avoid loitering members of the public, and City Hall staff, on the way.

One final bit of preamble to this long story, but a crucial one. The room being used for the court of which Stanley was chairman on the day was a committee room. There was a dais about six or nine inches high upon which the tables forming the bench were arranged. There was a door slightly behind and to the side of this dais, but it led only to a cleaners' store cupboard. So, unlike every other courtroom, the magistrates, when they needed to retire to confer in private, could not egress through a door behind or to the side of them to a retiring room of some sort. Instead, in this courtroom, when it was necessary for the magistrates to retire, the court clerk would as usual ask the court to rise, but instead of the magistrates departing as usual through an adjoining door, in this room the magistrates stayed in situ and everybody else filed out and waited in the corridor.

At last the story

I was on duty in the court at the top of the spiral staircase. On reflection things were quiet, I was idling or, like Sir Richard Grenville in Alfred Lord Tennyson's poem "The Revenge", laying at anchor. When "a pinnace like a flutter'd bird came flying from far away". In my case the "flutter'd bird" was an elderly, breathless, usher. What is more, he came from the court as far away from my then location as it was possible to be. Like the "flutter'd bird" of the poem, mine, in his flappy black usher's gown, brought calamitous news. Not, in my case, that he had sighted 53 Spanish ships (we were then over 50 miles from the nearest sea), but instead, a report that Stanley was puce with anger, and he needed the duty probation officer IMMEDIATELY.

So far as I knew no case, in the court which Stanley then chaired, was of any interest to our service on that day; so I was puzzled. I started to say this, but the usher was pleading with me to hurry. No doubt he felt that if he failed to get me before Stanley pronto that it would be he that then felt the wrath of the man. Given the usher's age and breathlessness I calculated that a minimum of four minutes had already expired since the summons so I decided to make a start, leaving the "flutter'd bird" in my wake.

Down the two spiral staircases, under number one court, up the long marble stairs and down the corridor to the court room in question. There was a pin drop silence as I entered. The terrified defendant looked at me nonplussed. A pretty smarmy solicitor looked at me in a supercilious way and the court clerk Brian (he of the three piece suit and watch with fob chain) smiled at me and briefly raised his eyes heavenward. Stanley then harangued me for fully three minutes. Fortunately for me, some of my training had been under Royal Naval Reserve discipline, and I had received my fair share of admonishments, and took it, as I had then learnt; back straight, feet together, thumbs down the seams of my trousers, and focus on a point at the end of the officer's nose. I was unable to make any sense of the complaint being given (it later transpired that Stanley had mistakenly focused on an alleged and unfounded complaint about the probation service made by the smarmy solicitor from a neighbouring city) and just had to get it off his chest and the probation officer of the day would do. The tirade ended. Stanley rose abruptly. Surprising his wingers, the two less senior magistrates allotted to sit with him that day. He moved swiftly behind the winger to his right, making no doubt for what he thought was the retiring room, to calm down having vented his spleen.

He yanked the door open and strode inside.

He disappeared from view to the various sounds of scattering metal pails, dust pans, brushes, intermingled with stifled oaths.

The wingers were stunned. The courtroom hushed.

Brian kept his cool.

"Clear the courtroom." he said.

*

Probation officers of the day would often refer to themselves as "officers of the court" and perhaps that is not surprising since we were, as I have shown, very much linked to the magistrates. But I believe that probation officers may never have technically been true "officers of the court". The real officers of the court in a formal sense are the barristers and solicitors who have legal qualification and through that automatic right of audience in court. Nevertheless it was perhaps reasonable for probation officers to feel that they were officers of the court, because of their peculiar link to magistrates as their employers and in the way the court required them to undertake so many jobs in their behalf. A dear friend and colleague, another Geoffrey, once made a list in the early 1970s of the duties of the probation officer of the day and it came in three parts, the first and second parts related to our work for different types of courts and the third part covered the work for other official bodies. I'm afraid I have lost the original but it went something like this:-

For the criminal courts – Magistrates, Quarter Sessions and Assizes:-

Social enquiry reports (later pre-sentence reports) on adults aged 18 and over.

Social enquiry reports on juvenile offenders aged 10 to 17 inclusive.

Supervision of persons subject to probation orders from the age of 10 upwards.

Progress reports to Case Committees and Courts on probationers.
Reports to the court where a probationer was in breach of the order.
Reports on disputes between neighbours.

For the Family Courts, both Magistrates and County:-
Reports concerning the custody of children.
Reports concerning the access to children.
Supervision of some access periods in difficult cases.
Adoption Guardian ad litem reports.
Reports on applications from minors to marry (the age of consent to marry was still 21 until 1970).

For penal institutions:-
Reports for Borstals and the supervision of those on licence about 12 months.
Reports for Detention Centres and the supervision of those on licence of three months.
Reports for Approved Schools and the supervision of those on after-care.
Reports for the parole board and the supervision of those on parole licence (from 1967).
Reports for prisons regarding the suitability of proposed home leaves.
Supervision of persons released from life imprisonment sentences.
Supervision of persons released from secure hospitals.

Clearly I am not sure that I am remembering all that was included in the original list my colleague made, but it clearly showed the breadth of the work. It was a helpful list to take out when doing talks to community groups. The list indicates the wonderful variety of our work, so far as I was concerned. The probation officer dealt in criminal work as their bread and butter, but as time had gone on they had been given many other duties for which the court record required a direct agent to act in their behalf. This was particularly evident in relation to family court work which continued to increase in the later 1960s and especially in the 1970s. Often these added duties, especially those relating to family work, might well have been categorised the probation officer role as social worker to the courts.

So the court orientation of the probation officer was clear; the magistrates in particular were well aware of the type, and the breadth of the work the officers did and there was ongoing regular contact between the representatives of the magistrates, namely probation committee members, and the officers. I suspect that, leaving aside the later drive of managerialism in the service, which sought internal control, there was also some jealousy from other services. The police, for example, were by the mid-1960s beginning to lose their contacts with the courts. In city areas like ours, with its own police and probation services serving the city alone, there were relatively few people involved. Magistrates amounted to about 300 divided into three rota's which sat once every three weeks. I would guess that the city police and staff were a lot higher in number but the local probation service only had about 60 all told including clerical staff. All the prosecutions were conducted by police staff in the magistrates' court up until the advent of prosecuting solicitors in the city in the late 1960s. Even then there were only a couple of prosecutors and police officers still prosecuted many matters. What is more police officers tended to give evidence in trials and so there were always officers in uniform around the court building.

So magistrates knew many police staff but there was no management connection between the magistracy and the constabulary.

Incidentally, as a slight digression, there was never any need for court security personnel in the 1960s since there were always officers in uniform able to deal with any issues which arose including issues of contempt of court. Contempt of court may be the defendant being abusive, but could also be members of the public who misbehave. Any such misbehaviour in those days could be dealt with by the prompt arrival of a police officer.

Forty years later I was on duty in a Crown Court where an incident occurred in the public area. The circuit judge issued a warning that the next outburst would result in the person he identified as being responsible for it would be taken to the cells in contempt of court. Nothing further happened, but later that day I had occasion to meet the judge about another matter and I enquired of him what the chances were of any miscreant in the public gallery actually being taken to the cells. His comment was that the chances were slim, since the civilian dock officers could not leave the prisoner and the only private court security staff were probably at the front door some two stories below the courtroom. The chances of a real police officer being anywhere within a mile of the building were quite low. Then, just a few years ago, I read in my local newspaper about a prisoner who escaped from the dock in that same Crown Court and was apprehended by the rugby tackle applied by a young court newspaper reporter.

The probation officer of the day was treated by the courts as "one of their officers", because the magistrates themselves were our employers and we did deal with a wide range of enquiries and duties on their behalf. It was more of a courtesy title than a truly legal one. In our role as supervisors of individual offenders on orders, but even more so in relation to our family work, we were also, quite clearly, social workers to the courts.

Chapter 4
Band of Brothers......and Sisters

"But we in it shall be remembered - we few, we happy few, we band of brothers;"
From *"Henry V"* by William Shakespeare (circa 1599)

*

The staff room was an important place in the office, especially for officers who, by the nature of the work, were working independently during the rest of day. It was a place to relax, hear stories from court and generally be off duty for a while. Lunchtime was a busy time, sandwiches were consumed, stories swapped and mild pranks undertaken. Colleagues trusting enough to leave packets of biscuits around would never find any missing (after all it would be wrong to indulge in theft), however, many would find the packet of the digestive or water biscuits they had purchased appeared to have suffered severe mishandling reducing them to crumbs before they were purchased - or was it afterwards!

One day we decided that an officer who had recently been promoted and was to leave us, and as a result had been a little uppity of late, might benefit from a little comedown. We removed the springs from one of the easy chairs and awaited his arrival, warning those not the target, to avoid the adapted chair. As luck would have it the target was late to lunch and we had taken our eye off the ball. Enter a matronly female colleague bearing a newspaper package of fish and chips (she was due to work late that evening).

Before any of us could intervene she sat in the adapted chair and as planned the cushion gave way. Down went her considerable posterior until, softened by the cushion, it reached the floor. Up went the fish and chips only to land on her extremely ample bosom. We flew to her aid explaining that this was not meant to be and offering to get her up.

"Leave me!" she roared, "I might as well eat these from the ledge where they have landed, and don't any of you dare to attempt to pinch one!"

*

Some of the trained staff, including myself, had previous employment experience and the variety of prior experience amongst the whole staff was huge. Except for two trained officers who had gone from school to training and straight into the job there were, amongst others, police officers, a district nurse, a district housing officer, a mental welfare officer, a dispensing chemist, a housewife, a maritime telegraphist, several Salvation Army captains, a regular Army WO 1 and a merchant seaman; the latter was me.

Already I have made reference to the equality of gender issue that was evident from the very inception of the service, namely that at least one man and one woman had to be appointed as probation officers in each local court. That gender equality was evident when I arrived in the city. Female staff made up over 40% of officers I would judge. Of the four senior officers one was female. And by the time I am writing about the prohibition on female staff supervising male offenders had been lifted and they were now entirely equal in role with male counterparts.

Having reflected upon the journey which led to the formation of the probation service I turn to a review of my own journey to join its ranks is. Why was I here?

My father and his work partner ran a successful small building business. I'm sure that he would have liked me to go into the business but it never appealed to me. Fortunately, from my perspective, there was a four generation family tradition of service at sea. My father, a time served carpenter and cabinetmaker, had worked as a ship's "chippy" or carpenter for several years in the 1930s when unable to get work ashore, his father had been a Bristol Channel pilot and his a dock pilot and his a fisherman. There was also the threat of National Service and I was not sure that one could choose the Navy over other services so I might not have ended up at sea (I was not averse to a Service life and later ended up as an R.N.R officer for a short while). One way of avoiding National Service was to be in the merchant navy and so at fifteen I left home for merchant navy training school, and thence to sea.

The first of life's lessons I learned at that early age was that living alongside other young men from a variety of backgrounds, and with unbelievably different morals and values, widened one's own horizons, along with one's eyes when you heard some of the tales told. This taught me to accept that my fellow human being is a complex character, capable of good and bad; but that in the main was capable of change. Mixing with my contemporaries changed my perspective. I suppose that higher education increasingly offered that opportunity after National Service declined. But as higher education was not open to all, perhaps there were many young people who were denied that important opportunity, to meet a cross-section of their fellows. I have long thought that a return to new and improved National Service could benefit young people. There could be opportunity to choose between a military aspect and a social service aspect where, in the latter case, young people gave service in a community, and did so under a disciplined structure and whilst living together with their fellows. Indeed there could be some who give service in developing countries, in lieu of our government giving cash to those nations where it would appear that the aid does not always effectively get to those in need.

That international element was prominent in a second major lesson, which came from my time in the merchant navy. Visiting the area then known as "the cages" in downtown Bombay, an area of great poverty, I was struck by the appalling conditions and the sight of handicapped and limbless beggars. This really impacted a teenager from the UK who had never seen the like in our society, where we had health and social services. It was also re-enforced, literarily half a world away, when I visited Sao Vicente, a port near Concepción in Chile, where again the poverty and the plight of children was so obvious.

So, disability, both physical and mental, together with the very different morals of those with whom I was thrown together, were issues with which I was confronted at an impressionable age. Also, in analysing one's own development, one must also look at the mores of the time as they play a part in the socialisation process.

Another subtle ingredient in my eventual arrival in the probation service was undoubtedly a television series which aired between 1959 and 1962 and was based on real-life probation cases. The show centred on the work of individual probation officers, men and women responsible for the supervision of offenders. "Probation Officer" was an ATV production and the first one-hour drama series to be carried on the ITV network, and it was very popular. I have no doubt that it had some influence on my later career choice, albeit I was at sea in the merchant navy for some of that period and would not have seen many episodes (No "catch up" in those days!).

I found that the merchant navy I had joined was an industry in decline. I had to get four years sea time, yes 365 days x 4 actually at sea, and shore leave did not count, before I was eligible to sit for my first navigation officer examinations, which I passed. As a result I got my ticket, or more formally, my Board Of Trade Certificate of Competency as Second Mate (Foreign Going). But I had already seen worrying developments in my chosen industry. The British owned merchant fleet was declining. Bigger ships meant less ships and therefore less need for officers to sail. Flags of convenience led to ships being registered in countries where standards were less stringent, and in turn opened the doors to seamen from other countries. The oversupply of qualified officers meant that promotion was stagnating. The time required in "waiting for dead men's shoes" was increasing, and my company had inserted an extra rank in the chain of command to try to give people some encouragement. But the writing was, it seemed to me, upon the wall.

My choice was twofold. To press ahead with getting my next two tickets, namely Mates and then Masters. This might have improved my employability ashore, but, to do so, required a further 3 years of sea time, by when I would have been in my later twenties. Alternatively, I could come ashore and start again in a new direction. I took the latter view and as the old seagoing adage goes, I "swallowed the anchor", in other words, left the sea for good.

What qualifications did I have? The aforementioned second mate's ticket was perhaps just a little more use than two of my three

General Certificates in Education (GCE) which were Seamanship and Navigation. (Dear reader I guess you did not know there were such GCE's). So English Language was my only useful shore side qualification. I had saved money at sea and there was a cushion, but I realised such funds would not last. My parents were kind enough to accommodate me, but they were in the process of retiring from west London to the south coast. Fortunately there was full employment at that time, and so within a week of my decision I was at work as a builder's labourer and van driver. Then, when I moved with my parents to the south coast I got a job as a storeman in a horticultural company. Both jobs improved my physical fitness; but sadly not my future prospects. Of course, chance plays a part in changing life's direction, and here came mine. An article appeared in the local paper, whereby the town Youth Officer was seeking someone with an interest in sailing, to volunteer to lead a group of young people at a youth club in restoring a sailing dingy. I contacted them and I got the job, not surprising since I was the only applicant.

One thing led to another, and soon I was a volunteer helper at the youth club two nights a week and the local council paid for me to attend some youth leadership training events. It was indicated to me that if I wished to go further in the youth service, or any related work, I would need more training and a precursor to that would be more formal academic qualifications. So it was work in the day, two evening evenings a week at youth club (now joint volunteer leader), and two nights a week at the local further education college.

More good luck then took a hand. Our youth club was to move to new premises in a former infant school which was itself moving to a new site. The plan was for it to be used as a centre for the elderly by day, and for a mixture of adult evening classes and youth clubs in the evening. They needed a part-time superintendent to manage it, and I applied for the post and got it. My role was to lead the evening youth work whilst the elderly persons' activities were coordinated by someone else, leaving me with the administration of the whole centre and also the time to go to the further education college in the day. The upshot of this left me with sufficient "O" and "A" levels to think about a career in the social work field.

In the early 1960's I applied to the Probation Department of the Home Office and was called for interview. There were three parts to the interview. The first was an intelligence test, a sort of Eleven-Plus exam for grown-ups (the Eleven-Plus was a selection test, started in 1944 to determine the academic level of a child in order to see if they were worthy of going to the grammar schools of the day – I had failed mine!). Then followed a group discussion, in which applicants sat with two probation inspectors and were required to contribute verbally to a set topic. Then an individual interview followed, and, for me, that was with Miss Molly Samuels a lady who remained in post for many years and whom I met again much later in my career; she was a most well-respected Probation Inspector of the day.

To my delight the Home Office agreed to sponsor me in my studies. This meant they paid the course fees and gave me a grant towards living expenses. I secured a place in the Department of Social Administration at Hull University on a two-year course leading to the Diploma in Social Administration. Not a degree course.

My tutor was Warren Fox and the course leader Bessie Raine, and in my humble opinion they ran an excellent course. As well as the academic inputs there was plenty of 'hands on' experience. A two-week taster in the probation office in Eastbourne; one month with a prison probation officer at HMP Ford open prison; two months in a voluntary social services organisation dealing with the elderly and two months in a mental welfare office at Huddersfield Council.

After two years and gaining the diploma there was a further year on the Applied Diploma in Social Administration which was the professional qualification of the day for entry into social work. Here too there was a lot of practical work. Two long placements of three months each, first at the Children's Department of Scarborough Council, on a two day per week concurrent placement and the second, a mainly full time placement at the Probation Office in New Cross Street, Hull

At the end of all this I reached the point of looking for work which led to the experience as described in chapter 1.

Chapter 5
Learning the Ropes

In the days of sailing ships, especially on large vessels with many sails, there were countless ropes with different functions for setting and trimming the sails and getting the best out of the ship. Any new recruit would therefore have to spend time learning the location and function of each rope – hence 'learning the ropes'. This nautical term came ashore and is still applied to many learning experiences.

*

"Come on, we have to pick up an ill patient from the general hospital and transport him to a psychiatric unit", said my placement supervisor in the mental welfare office.

In the 1960s, people working in social work were specialised into different services. Probation Officers worked with offenders and hospital almoner's worked with patients in hospital. Then, local councils were responsible for other social work services; through Children's Departments with Child Care Officers; housing and general welfare services with Housing and Welfare Officers and then for mental health services in the community Mental Welfare Officers. Services attracted people with a particular interest in the type of work and the clientele with which the service dealt. In my experience many mental welfare officers of the time had a great concern for all their clients, but many were extremely outgoing and able to tailor their responses, in an easy going and non-threatening way, to clients who were locked in worlds or moods of their own. Thus, some developed, what I can only describe as a cheerful and carefree exterior. This was true during my placement in a mental welfare office.

We arrived at the local general hospital to collect the patient who, it transpired, was being seen by a doctor. My supervisor told me to wait in the corridor and went off in discussion with two burly white coated male nurses. I was looking out of the window when the two nurses came up and grabbed my arms and took me onto the ward, easily overpowering my mild yet confused resistance, and strained explanations that I was not ill. To which they replied "It's all right son, they all say that, but we will make you better soon".

It was a set up by my supervisor, for a bit of fun for him and the nurses. I suppose that the work was so often difficult there was a need to let off steam when one could.

I never forgot those few seconds of loss of liberty, that feeling of having lost control of one's own life, and they informed my dealing with offenders over the years to follow. And it was particularly relevant, many years later, when I sat for nine years hearing the appeals against their detention of 'sectioned' mental patients.

*

In the previous chapter, and in this example, I refer to the opportunities to practice under supervision whilst on placements. What about the theory? What then was the academic content of the two courses which qualified me professionally as a probation officer?

Although taught disparately there were two essential elements that were covered. Firstly, there were those subjects which focussed upon aspects of society which surrounded, influenced or constrained the individual. Secondly, there were those things which formed or influenced the development of that particular individual, and the way they functioned.

I will first deal with those subjects which clearly fall into that first element of societal factors surrounding the individual and then go on to those which either straddle both elements or are clearly in the second.

Social History.

Understanding history, particularly recent history, is crucial to understanding the present. It is now some years since I celebrated my anniversary of reaching the biblical milestone of threescore years and ten. The person I am now is very different to how I was as a young man. Many of these changes have come about from life experience leading to greater understanding, but others have come about because of the change of social mores. As a simple example I would refer to the fact that I have managed to (mainly) rid myself of many of the words which were in common parlance and usage in the 1950s, and which are today deemed unacceptable.

Thus it was, that social history was felt to be a significant area of study in order to discover why we had reached the point we had in the development of social services. The main focus was on the developments of the period between 1850 and the birth of the welfare state some 90 years later.

We looked at developments from the Poor Law, through the growth of the charity movement of the second half of the 1800s and into the twentieth century. Then we looked at the social changes brought about via the catalyst of the First World War. Finally we considered the issues leading to the development of the Welfare State after the Second World War.

Social Administration.

Following on from the study of social history we moved on to looking at the structures that were in place to deliver welfare in that post-war period. In linking social history to social administration I found that one book of 1961, which, incidentally, is still in my bookcase, entitled "The Coming of the Welfare State" by Maurice Bruce, was particularly helpful. My notes suggest that he may have argued that the welfare state of that time grew out of the needs of English society and also out of the struggle for social justice. Furthermore, that beginning with the Poor Law and later by other means there was an acceptance of community responsibility for less fortunate members of society. Then as society developed and became more self-conscious there was a widening both of the areas of responsibility and the range of services provided.

I have already referred to the different departments of local authorities that delivered social work services to the community. However, social administration included a whole range of welfare provision including the financial support delivered by the Social Security service. It was felt imperative for the practising social worker to be fully aware of the work of all these different departments, how they were managed, how they operated, and how social work clients could access their different services.

It will be seen from my earlier comments that not only did we receive theoretical instruction about these matters, but before I qualified I had actually worked under supervision in a Children's Department, a Mental Welfare Department, a Welfare Department working with the elderly and in a prison setting. By and large, my learning and experience showed me that staff in these different settings were extremely well versed in their roles and responsibilities, and often people were attracted to one service or another by the nature of the department's work. Interestingly, after my training had completed the Seebohm Report was implemented in the early 1970s. This required all social workers to stop working in specialised areas, to become generic and to undertake the whole range of work.

I merely comment that to the casual observer of today's services that social worker genericism appears, ironically, itself been replaced by a return to specialism.

Law

Our law lecturer was Professor Bevan, a much respected, and published, legal academic. He had a catchphrase which appealed to me and which served me well throughout my career. "You do not need to know the Law, just where to look it up". In those years before the internet this was sound and helpful advice.

The range and detail of the information provided was considerable. My notes on A4 paper run to about 50 sheets; written double sided. We covered the structure of the criminal courts, how cases proceeded through them, the sentences available and how those sentences were managed by those responsible, in the main that was the prison and probation services. There was then matrimonial law, which of course in those days was predicated on an adversarial system where one party was seeking to show that the other party was at fault. We learnt about the law on adoptions and guardianship, and even the law as it related to each of the different agencies responsible for social work provision including the Department of Social Security.

Then there was very detailed work on the law relating to probation orders. Again I made copious notes which were invaluable to me years later, when I myself was responsible for training probation officers at a later stage in my career.

As I previously indicated some of the taught subjects straddled the two elements of societal and individual influences, and I would place the following subjects in this latter category.

Sociology

This was taught on the basis that it was an important area of study for coming to an understanding of how man is inseparable from his environment, i.e. the society in which he finds himself, and of how during the process of socialisation he comes to develop a sense of identity which governs his interactions with others.

We heard how anthropologists such as Mead and Eriksson offered an analysis as to how socialisation occurs and that Caplan had enumerated three areas of need which an individual requires from society for normal development and interactions to take place, but which can result in conflict and deviance if inadequately met. Then Parsons who saw the function of the family as vital in assisting the socialisation process, this being achieved through positive attachments to a parent or carer. Also covered was child development from infancy, through adolescence to adult-hood. Finally, consideration was given to the problems of deviance from accepted normative standards and of deviant subcultures within a given society.

Psychology

We studied psychology on the basis that it provided pointers to help understand an individual's behaviour, which, as Freud believed, can be determined on both the conscious and unconscious level. In the unconscious, as a sense of right and wrong steadily develop through socialisation, the individual needs a means of burying unacceptable things so as to maintain his internal stability. This is done by employing defence mechanisms, which help the individual to defend themselves from acknowledging the desires and actions they experience, yet which they have learned are unacceptable in their society. We were referred to Caplan's book "An Approach to Community Mental Health" where he considered an individual's ability to respond to crises and how a healthy mother child relationship from infancy was conducive to mental stability.

In the 1960s the idea of maternal deprivation as put forward by Bowlby in his "Childcare and the Growth of Love" was in vogue. Although it was later seen as an oversimplification of the need for close bonds with the mother in the early years as other caring adults can also fulfil this role.

Then Eriksson in his "Identity, Youth and Crisis" pointed to adolescence being particularly challenging for an individual's development sometimes leading to a crisis of identity, such as peer pressures outweighing familial influences. And Anna Freud in her book "Ego and the Mechanisms of Defence" suggested that certain defences are linked to certain psychiatric illnesses.

Mental Ill-Health

As mental ill-health may also be a factor in some deviant behaviour it too was covered. We were told there were two groups of mental health ill-health issues, ones with an organic basis due to a bodily disorder or impairment and ones with a psychological basis including neuroses and psychoses.

Neuroses, such as anxiety and depression, we learned were disorders of emotion or intellectual functioning which do not deprive the individual of contact with reality. Psychotic illnesses, however, such as schizophrenia, propel the patient into an unreal world and often lead to a progressive deterioration of the entire personality.

One of the big talking points of the day related to the psychopathic personality. Two categories were outlined, those who were aggressive and those who were inadequate; although there was an overlap, we were told, between each. All psychopaths were seen as emotionally immature, impulsive, unreliable and seeking short-term gains which may lead from one disaster to another as they are incapable of learning from experience. Psychopaths were seen as being unable to fit into society

Finally, in addition to all these topics, we studied Social Casework.

In short, this was defined as a method of assessment of individual functioning with a view to formulating how specific behaviours might be changed. Essentially, at least in part, Social Casework was the accepted method of intervention of the time, based upon a disease model and as such is worthy of a section of its own.

Chapter 6
Social Casework

"Social casework is the art of bringing about better adjustment in the social relationship of individual men or women or children"
From *"What is Social Casework"* by Mary E Richmond (1922)

*

Bill was a young man from a very dysfunctional family; all of the males including the father had been in trouble with the law. When he came on probation I knew it would be very difficult for me to meaningfully engage him in any work. And so it proved. For over six months of his probation order he did nothing but, what we used to call, "kick the table leg". By this is meant, that he used to keep his appointments, but when he came he would be monosyllabic, and try as I might I could not get him to engage in any meaningful discussions. Of course, on one level he was obeying his order. He turned up when he was told to and there was nothing in the order which said he had to talk to me. At the end of each interview he would ask me for the bus fare home, which I routinely refused, since he lived less than 2 miles from the office and in any event it was not policy to give bus fare save in exceptional circumstances.

It was my practice to get into the office early. That glorious hour between eight and the office switchboard and door opening to the public at nine, was critical in my being able to keep up-to-date with my paper work. One morning, however, just after eight there was a tap on my window and there stood Bill, my monosyllabic probationer, who was obviously emotionally very upset. I went to the office door unlocked it and, letting him in locked it again, and took him into my office.

His story, which came tumbling out, was that he had been in his local public house the previous evening when an altercation occurred and a young man with whom he was sitting got into a fight with another man which resulted in this second person being stabbed to death. Bill had been with the police all night giving a critical witness statement of the events. He was emotionally drained, and still somewhat in shock. I allowed him to talk and he must have done so for the best part of an hour. On his way out I offered him the bus fare home.

Subsequently, our relationship improved and he was regularly able to talk to me about a variety of issues.

The book "Fate is the Hunter" by Earnest K. Gann, refers in one part to the amazing avoidance of a mid-Atlantic aviation disaster by an airline pilot deciding, out of mid-flight boredom, to lower his cruising altitude by just 50 feet to exactly match the prescribed altitude in the flight plan. Seconds after completing the manoeuvre, an aircraft flying at the wrong altitude in the opposite direction passes just 50 feet above him. Fate he says took a hand in that.

Fate can also take a hand in changing human relationships, as in my description of the changed relationship with Bill. But changes can also be made by analysing what has to change, and planning how to do it. Essentially this latter underpins the ethos of social casework.

*

My training course looked at the history of the development of social casework which really began in the early 1900s and moved on to the ideas of social casework practice as they were understood in the late 1950s and very early 1960s.

The development of psychiatry gathered pace in the 1800s and as social work practice developed it took a lot of its principles from psychiatry. The American, Mary E. Richmond, was an outstanding early social casework practitioner, teacher, and theoretician who formulated the first comprehensive statement of principles of direct social work practice in books such as "Social Diagnosis" (1917) and "What is Social Casework" (1922). Interestingly she provided one of the early definitions of social work; "Social casework is the art of bringing about better adjustment in the social relationship of individual men or women or children" from "What is Social Casework" by Mary E Richmond (1922)

As social work practice developed others began to try to define what it was. In 1957 Father Beistek, an American priest who studied sociology, and later became a professor of social work, published his book "The Casework Relationship". In it he developed his 'principles of casework', and my notes suggest he identified seven:-
- Treating each client as a distinct individual.
- Allowing clients the opportunity to fully express their feelings.
- Not getting emotionally involved with clients.
- Accepting the client and his views, whatever the worker may feel about them.
- Not making personal judgements about them.
- Accepting that the client has the right to self-determination.
- Confidentiality.

The most up to date theorist whose work was taught on our last course was Florence Hollis who saw social casework as a method used by social workers to aid individuals to find solutions to problems of social adjustment which they were unable to manage on their own.

In her work Hollis was primarily influenced by Sigmund Freud's psychoanalytic theory and Mary Richmond's casework theory. The main ideas in her casework theory were acceptance, relationship, empathy, listening, reassurance, encouragement, self-determination, the importance of talking in treatment, expressions of feelings in treatment, workers self-knowledge, diagnosis and training in social work. In a way Hollis was firmly grounded in social work principles that drew quite heavily on psychoanalytic theory as a means of understanding human behaviour.

Chapter 7
Social Caseworker

"Physician heal thyself". (Luke 4;23)

*

It was office closing time and I had been on duty seeing casual callers to the office that afternoon. As part of that duty it was my job to close the front door to the public at office closing time. It had been a very busy, even stressful, day and I felt under pressure as I was due to make a home visit on an urgent matter which I had scheduled for half an hour after the office was due to shut. As I approached the front door a man came in who was obviously the worse for drink. Now I had a lot of experience with drunks from my time at sea. When you could hear a raucous, drunken crew on its way back to the ship from a night on the Reeperbahn in Hamburg at 0200 hours, the second mate used to say to the apprentice (me) 'see that crowd gets to their bunks without trouble'. Then he would magically disappear I learned from that experience to take your time, keep your voice down and not be confrontational.

At any other time I would have taken my time and talked him out of the door. Today however, my mind was on the need for haste, and I handled it all wrong.

His request was for money but almost before the request had left his lips I went into the mode of telling him no chance, the office was closed, come back tomorrow and on your way. This immediately set up a confrontation and we both became aggressive towards one another in a verbal sense. The situation was only resolved by a long-time colleague who intervened took the heat out of the situation and eventually was able to persuade the visitor to leave, empty-handed.

Within minutes I was in my colleagues office in tears. I was not much given to this sort of behaviour during my working life but on this occasion I was really upset. I was not upset with the man, the fact that he was asking for money, the fact that he was late, but more I was upset with myself for having failed to deal with the matter in the way that I normally would have done. Just because of a stressful day and being focused on the fact of getting to my appointment provided no justification for not acting professionally. The tears were frustration, with myself.

*

My training took place on a course which had, as well as students with no particular attachment to any type of social work, a large proportion of students seeking to get professional qualifications but who were already in employment in social work, as in fact was the case of my wife to be. There were a goodly number from children's departments, from voluntary organisations and, like me, from the probation service. We learnt, as can be seen, about a variety of things which would assist us in our work as social caseworkers, but were we really suited to fulfil that role?

One of the tenets of social casework that we were taught was the understanding of oneself. So who was I and what did I have to recognise about myself when undertaking work with clients.

In chapter 4, above, I described the practical chronology of my starting out on the road to become a probation officer. But what were my underlying values and traits and how would they inform, help or hinder my work.

Already I have alluded to the importance of history in understanding the present. In my own development the mores of the time in which I grew up played a big part in my socialisation process. In the late 1940s and 1950s religious values were still strong in our society. My parents were officially non-practising Church of England, but their own upbringings were seated in Christian values. Mum in the local parish church, in which her brother was a choirboy and my dad in the chapel culture of South Wales. So both my parents had clear moral values drawn from their experience in these institutions. They passed those values on to me and when I was about twelve or so, I decided for a while, to go to church on Sunday, on my own, and also to participate in church activities for the young. I did not continue that church membership, although I do occasionally attend a church service these days. Added to this was the clear Christian element in the state schools which I attended and I do find comfort even today in hearing and singing the better-known and loved traditional hymns which played a large part in school religious 'services'.

What I took from these Christian teachings was an understanding that we are all responsible for our own moral judgements in life. That, for example, we should not steal, or seek to do one's neighbour down, but at the same time there should be an element of forgiveness, both for us in our failures and others in theirs. Whilst the history of religion is littered with its own big failures, the Crusades and Inquisition for example, I feel that the Christian religion has become more gentle over the years. For me that is a sign of its maturity. In turn my own maturity came about from a benign Christian base tempered later by living cheek by jowl with a cross section of my fellow man and on top of that seeing, at an early and impressionable age, the plight and disadvantage of so many in other cultures.

Whether or not my status as an only child, to an older mother, had an impact, can only be a subject of conjecture. In my case I felt it gave rise to my developing a very independent nature, one which meant that I had little need for close friends and was quite happy in my own company. This in turn made me able to keep other people at arm's length, if required. If you like, I was able to maintain a distance when required.

Professional distance is, in my view, a crucial element for the caseworker. You must always be in control of yourself and your emotions, and that is why recounting the experience, with the drunk, at the start of this, is so painful. Fortunately there were few such experiences, if there had been more I would have been in the wrong job. You must be able to hear and empathise with client's issues; sometimes these were very intimate or personal details. You must see clients in a wholly asexual way and ensure all proper bounds of propriety. Despite the injunction to "befriend" clients, that was, as I will later discuss, part of the probation ethos of the day, that friendship must be on a simple, almost superficial level, otherwise you could become personally involved; and that was a non-starter.

One of my personal techniques was to always be "Mr" to the clients. Yes, it could be seen to be over-bearing, but to me it was a manifestation of the difference in roles. I could befriend the client but only because we had been thrown together by the courts. I needed to make it clear that it was so, and the client also needed to be constantly aware of this fact.

Building on these factors I took to the elements of social casework such as being non-judgemental, keeping professional distance, keeping confidentiality and accepting the client as (s)he is. It also fitted me that I was entering a role where I was working as an independent professional, making my own judgements and taking personal responsibility for my work. I also had a clear understanding of what was right and wrong and, where there was something that was beyond the pale, I could be strong in ensuring that the client surrendered themselves to the relevant authority or, if they failed to do so, I was comfortable in reporting them.

Another factor that was to help me in my work as a social caseworker was that I was passably good with words (though, dear reader, you may opine otherwise) and control of vocabulary was an asset in the social work process. Furthermore, some experience in minor thespian roles also gave me confidence in speaking in a public setting, and in turn this enabled me to offer courts clear assessments of my clients' situations when that was required.

Chapter 8
Transition

"You must be the change you wish to see in the world."
Mahatma Ghandi

*

In the 1960s there were relatively few stipendiary magistrates, they were legally trained and were appointed in large courts to help with the volume of business. They usually sat alone. There was one in the Hull Magistrates Court at the time I commenced my final four-month training placement in probation in that city. My first court duty there saw him deal swiftly with a number of the overnight arrests. However, he had a personal issue, to do with his apparently diminished hearing, as he frequently said "speak up" to solicitors appearing before him. My mentor on the day told me that he was quite hard of hearing and that sometimes unrepresented prisoners in the dock, some distance from the bench, were inaudible to him. At which point the regular dock officer an ageing and rotund police officer, nicknamed by my colleague as "The Voice", would boom out verbatim the reply which the defendant had made, and which had not been received by the Stipe.

Enter a dishevelled male prisoner, obviously sobering up after a night in the cells, to face a charge of trespassing in an enclosed yard, and he was clearly not a happy chappie. When asked by the court clerk he replied "guilty". Being unrepresented, he was then asked if he had anything he wished to say about the offence. He muttered a reply, audible to those of us with undiminished hearing, but not well enough for the Stipe. I held my breath, thinking; surely The Voice cannot possibly repeat that in public.

Dear reader you should be aware that in a court where quoted words are to be used in evidence they must be verbatim so if you are of the sensitive nature or easily offended please miss out the next three lines

The Stipe said, "What did he say" looking at The Voice, who boomed out verbatim (as I had already heard) "The defendant states that 'he only went in for a bloody piss'".

There were a few coughs in the public gallery and the Stipe moved quickly to impose a fine.

*

So began the final hurdle in my attempt to qualify as a probation officer. The final examinations which had included papers on Human Growth and Development, Social Work, Law and Social Administration, were over. Only the results left to await. And now I embarked upon a four month final placement. My tutor was Frank, a Senior Probation Officer who ran a Home Office Training Unit which was situated within the Hull Probation Office in New Cross Street, but operated under the aegis of the Home Office. There were six of us in placement at one time. I should add here that the options for supervised placements were twofold. Either, like me, you went to a specialist unit, or alternatively you were assigned to an individual officer who had "volunteered" to be a supervisor on a one-to-one basis.

Many years later I found myself running one of these units and I very much felt that they were the best option, on average. Firstly the supervisor was full-time in the role of monitoring and helping the student to learn and progress, and second they were interested, and / or, skilled in teaching and third because with six trainees at any one time, by sharing experiences, it quickly built up expertise in many of the difficult situations that arise. Experiences could be shared and all of the students could learn from the experience of one of their number even if they did not experience the issue directly.

However, in later years, when asked by students coming to see me about the possibility of a placement, which type would I recommend as the best, I usually conceded that if you got an individual supervisor who had the interest and ability to teach and also had been given some workload relief then you may feel that they were the best bet. The trouble was that you could not be sure you would get all those ducks lined up in a row. An individual supervisor might not be good because their workload was too high, or they were reluctant supervisors because they had been "persuaded" they should take on this work, or even worse they saw it is good to have a student on supervision on the old *Curriculum Vitae*, but they really were basically not that interested in doing the job.

Three days after I started in the placement in the Hull office I made my first of what, during my whole career, must have been thousands of home visits to people's homes. Three days after that I interviewed a man also called Frank for my very first social enquiry report, which involved the case of Social Security fraud. A couple of weeks after that I attended Hull Magistrates Court where Frank was made subject of the first probation where I had written the report and where I also undertook the first part of the Order's s supervision.

An analysis of my caseload over the first two months of my placement showed that I had a caseload of 12 of which nine were on probation, one on licence from Borstal, one discharged prisoner requesting help and one matrimonial case. My youngest case was just 11 years old and at 34 the discharged prisoner was my oldest.

Cases came in two ways. Officers in the probation teams in Hull would refer cases to the students to supervise, or else you accrued new cases where the order had been made where you yourself had written the report. Towards the end of the placement, orders would be passed back to Hull officers. Because of the time constraints you got new or transferred cases in as soon as possible, hence I was up to 12 in the first half of my placement, and thereafter you took more report writing work and where the resulting cases were probation orders then the supervision went straight to local officers. Inevitably there was a tension in this exchange. Just before the students arrived there was pressure on local staff to give up some new orders. They may have done the report and felt they would have liked to supervise the case, but, were encouraged to hand it over to a "bloody student". Even worse was where the student had done the report and proposed probation in a case where the local officer felt that it should not have been. I was not aware of the flak Frank the supervisor probably got at the time, but when I undertook the role he then filled, some years later, I certainly found out.

Frank was a good teacher. He guided me through my placement in a calm and encouraging way. Like every teacher he had strong points and in his case it was the use of language, as I recall. He would pull both the content and language of my reports apart, but in doing so would clearly explain why. I welcomed this as I personally had grown up reading a lot. Not, you understand, the classics, but children's authors like Arthur Ransome whose prose was that of the early half of the 20th century and was therefore very grammatical and proper, 'never end with a preposition', and all that. The reader will clearly see how I've declined in that regard.

Looking back it was really a most positive experience. There was a knowledgeable, helpful and encouraging supervisor and a small group of other students in the same boat as myself. This latter aspect was a really important difference for those in a unit as opposed to those with individual supervisors. There were weekly opportunities for group discussions meaning that you learnt from your contemporaries' experiences as well as your own. Learning from this, I tried when I became a unit supervisor, to open up such discussion groups to students assigned to individual officers in my local office as well as my own, to assist both them and their hard pressed supervisors.

Whatever trade or profession you enter through a period of training you should be gaining confidence and competence, to the point where you feel ready for flying the nest. It all relied on the final placement report, the examination results had been okay, and I had therefore passed the course so long as Frank said I had passed the placement.

I later went on to supervise 52 students as a unit supervisor. Writing the final report was never easy. One had to assess a number of elements; the ability to relate to and supervise clients, the ability to evaluate information in order to write reports and plan how to work with clients, the ability to convey information in reports to the courts; to name but a few. In the main however, the assessment was an ongoing one, and for about 45 of my students the outcome became clear long before the need to write the report. They had clearly displayed the competences required; one simply had to adduce the salient points. The other seven had been made aware, from as early in the placement as was possible, that they had certain weaknesses and these, in true casework fashion, were identified and targets for change set.

Writing those latter reports was hard. There was a balance to be struck. Had the student heeded the need to improve in identified areas? To what extent had they improved? Was that improvement sufficient? Eventually, of the seven I passed four, and three of them went on to make successful careers as valued members of the service. One I guess I got wrong, in that he failed his probationary year following training. Of the three who did not pass, two accepted that they had not done enough to pass. One, however, accused me of bias and took his case to an examination board at his university where he, and I, each gave our evidence and he cross-examined me. The board decided that he had not passed his placement.

Frank's report on my performance was satisfactory and that information came a week or so before the end of the placement and I could look forward to that job that I had been offered as described earlier.

So, I was ready for flying the nest, but as fledglings the world over know, this action is fraught with unknown difficulties. You have tested your wings and know how they work but at the point of the first take-off you have a momentary anxiety about what the future really holds.

Anyway; that nice lady with a hat in chapter one had given me a job. So I had better get to it.

Chapter 9
Individual Case Management

"Start by doing what is necessary; then do what is possible; and suddenly you are doing the impossible." St Francis of Assisi.

*

My first office environment was, shall I say, interesting. The office was on three floors in a converted warehouse. When I say converted, I actually mean that the large open warehouse floors had been subdivided very cheaply by the use of some poor quality tentis boards, which have a straw coloured core. They were most certainly not soundproof. And this was a particular problem with my office, which was next to a staff toilet. Many is the time that, a critical or emotional point in an interview, the chain was pulled, followed by cascading water sounds. Or, even worse, the next door user suffered a loud bout of flatulence.

In fairness I did have an office of my own on the ground floor and it had a window which was barred on both sides and therefore impossible to clean, and the room was fairly dark even at midday because the wall of the adjoining warehouse building was just over one vehicle width away, across a cobbled alleyway. The entrance to the office was down that very same broken cobbled alleyway. You were then directed by a sign up a stairway to a reception desk, inconveniently situated on the first floor. So to visit me on a first occasion, the person would ascend the stairs, to be told by the receptionist to retrace their steps to the bottom turn right into the passageway come into the waiting area and my door was first on the left. It is not surprising that, on their second and subsequent visits, people wanting to see me would cut out the middleman and go straight to my door and knock. One never knew, when opening the door, whether one would be confronted with a nervous 11-year-old schoolboy, newly placed on probation, or a hulking aggressive drunk.

One of the drunks on my caseload (Billy Hall, the case study in Appendix 1) was so fed up with me being out one day, when he had called on the off chance, that he urinated on my door, I was informed by a disgruntled colleague.

This action somewhat inverts the suggestion that being fed up is, in the vernacular, being pissed off.

In his case, the fact that he was pissed off, led to my door being pissed on.

*

In true social casework terms of the day the individual case was managed by the taking of a social history, the planning of work to be done, with subsequent reviews, and recording everything relevant in the case. I know this must be true, because this is how the recording system was set up by Home Office decree. Records came in three parts.

Part A was on A3 paper folded to make a four sided form on the front of which were recorded the basic details of the person, full name, date of birth, address, and etcetera. Also there was recorded the index offence for which they were to be supervised. Then it recorded the full details of the requirements of the order. On the inside pages was room for details of the person's educational record and achievements their employment history and skills and also their list of previous convictions. The back page contained the social history of the person. Often, this was something that was contained in the report which led to the order being made, but not always since courts, especially the higher courts, in those days, did make orders without reports being done and even without reference to the probation service at all.

Perhaps a digression is required here to applaud the clerical staff of the day; yes clerical not administrative. In the modern age of word processing it is easy to forget that just one working lifetime ago we were still in the land of the typewriter and carbon paper. Even worse was the requirement to type onto 'Banda paper' this was a waxy based A4 sheet which cut a sort of stencil that could be passed through a 'Banda machine' which enabled several copies of a report to be produced. The problem was that you could not easily erase mistakes and when there were too many errors for comfort the poor clerical person had to start again.

So all these part A's had to be inserted into a typewriter and entries made; copied, in the main, from handwritten notes produced by officers. I think we had about seven clericals for the whole office and their day was almost exclusively typing. For the social history part, which usually meant about a page of typeface, we sometimes did cut-and-paste from the report.

The cutting was with scissors.

The pasting was with glue.

Part B was sometimes referred to as the "thinking sheet". Essentially it was a place where you made an assessment of the client's situation and identified the issues that needed to be addressed in order to reduce the likelihood of further offending. This plan was ideally shared with the client so that they were a party to what was to be done during the first three months of supervision. At this point, and at every subsequent quarterly point, the work was reviewed and an appropriate entry made, again involving the client.

I have started to use the term client to describe the probationer or supervisee. This was common parlance in probation and social work of the day. The definition of the word has, I think broadened, in the ensuing years and is often used in a business sense to describe the users of any business. I suggest that in the 1960s and 70s it more related to someone accessing a professional service, like a lawyer, physician, accountant or other independent professional, and the other ingredient was that there was a personal relationship between these people. In those days, as I have demonstrated, the probation officer was an individual responsible to the probation committee for their work, with limited line management, so very much the independent professional. Furthermore the work done was almost exclusively done on a one-to-one basis. The most obvious contemporary parallel is the work of a personal counsellor, so it was appropriate for the term client to be used.

To me it is telling that as we moved into the period after the probation order ended, which was from 1992, the term client gradually declined.

Ideally the part B would write itself where the person came onto probation via a social enquiry report. In those cases the good report would outline the reasons why the order was needed, in effect the assessment, then go on to broadly cover the work that was likely to be done. The report, in good practice, should be read by the offender prior to the court appearance so that they were aware what they were agreeing to do, if the order was made and they became a client. Indeed my practice was to invite the offender to attend my office to read the report before accompanying them to court. It was best to do this to ensure that they would agree in court to the probation order being made.

And they did have to agree to being placed on probation.

When probation as a sentence was swept away by the Criminal Justice Act 1991, not only did it begin to change the nomenclature of the persons supervised by probation officers from "client" to "offender" and subsequently "service user", it also dispensed with the requirement for the prospective probationer to agree to the making of an order for supervision. The idea of having to agree went back prior to the inception of the idea of probation orders, namely that there was a contract between the court, the offender and, in those experimental days before probation orders appeared on the statute book, a third party who undertook to work with the offender to try to ensure adherence to the terms of the order. Once probation orders existed then that third-party was the probation officer.

But surely it was Hobson's choice for an offender, standing in the dock, it is argued, for if they refused then surely they open themselves up to worse punishment, like prison for example. Well first it was not entirely unusual for the making of probation orders to be refused by offenders. It happened most frequently where offenders were fed up with their lives and were wanting to go to prison to escape the pressures and responsibilities of life in the community, and incidentally leaving those pressures and responsibilities, more often than not, to their dependants. "Partners" had not been invented in the 1960s the terms then were wife, spouse or cohabitee. But to me the importance of the need to consent related to the fact that the offender was agreeing to the outline of the work to be done, and expressing a willingness to do it. Of course some, even many, were just paying lip service, but even then you could return them to the point that this was the contract they had agreed to, at the making of the order, and that is what we must continue to focus on doing. Thus, to an extent, more limited in some cases than others, there was a hope that the client felt part of the process and thereby possibly more engaged.

The final part of the recording process, the Part "C", was the ongoing record sheet of every contact with the offender. I do mean every. Visits to the office (OV), home (HV), letters to and, less usually, from, the client, letters to and from third parties and telephone calls. Also, sadly in many cases, court appearances on new matters.

In later years after the demise of the probation order, computers came in and recording was then done by the officer, and typist/clerical of earlier years transmogrified into administrators. But, back in my first office, the typists struggled to type up the contacts. As an officer you could write out longhand the entries to be put onto the typed sheets by the typist, or you could use an early form of Dictaphone. These poor women, for the typists were all of that gender, had to contend with either varied and variable handwriting, or else, audio type from the Dictaphones. It is not much of a surprise that the Dictaphone entries were often more fulsome than the written ones. Indeed for those of us trained young social workers, with our casework theory very much to the fore, some interviews which were, to us, significant, could be recorded fully and one interview might cover a typed page.

So, the social work model of record keeping was central to my work as I took up my first post, and indeed, it was the cornerstone of the work I did with clients. Of course there was support and guidance from my senior probation officer, George, but his role in relation to my cases was primarily to do with helping me to evaluate the work I was doing with the clients. I felt very much like an independent professional consulting with my more experienced older colleague. We had serious professional exchanges about cases and their management and in many ways there was the familiarity of careful case evaluation that had been experienced and encouraged in my training. What George was more important in helping me with was twofold, adjusting to new timescales and to the volume of work.

In training timescales were short. The final professional qualifying course was 11 months and there were two placements both of four months, but the first one was only two days per week. So whilst you got a flavour of the work, you knew that in a very short time you would be moving on. Now, I was faced with a much different timescale. Once an order was made for two years or in some cases three, I would supervise them from start to finish. Indeed some cases lasted much longer as people would reoffend and new orders would be made. It was not unusual for a client to be seeing you relatively often for four or five years. Then of course for those who completed an order a new offence months or years later would bring them your way again.

In our city office the rules were clear. Once you picked up a client then it was usual for you to deal with them from that point forward. Whether there was a report to write, or an order to supervise, then you picked the matter up unless there were sound professional reasons not to do so. I can think of a large number of clients with whom I dealt over decades. The only way you could move your caseload round was to move to a different area. A lot of my early colleagues chose this option.

It so happened I worked in the same city for 34 years.

But just as timescales were a new thing to adjust to, so was the volume of work. I mentioned earlier that in training after two months I had 12 cases, but on arrival I inherited 40 cases from an officer who had left, and was to boot, an officer who believed in seeing the clients and not doing the records. There were a number of those I seem to recall. To add insult to injury, these cases were not in the area where I was destined to work. The city boundary, vaguely circular in shape, was divided into four quadrants at the time, north-east, where I was destined to work, south-east where the inherited cases lived, south-west and north-west.

Working in smaller geographical areas allowed officers to become familiar with the local communities and to forge links with the relevant institutions which, so far as we were concerned were principally the secondary schools and the social work departments, especially children's and mental welfare. It also cut travelling time when out on the patch. In those days a lot of work was done in clients' homes, where you could also have contact with the significant others in their lives. So for schoolchildren it was the parents, and for adults, marriage partners or cohabitees.

So, how to manage these new issues became a big part of supervision which I welcomed. I was grateful to George for his help in these matters. Also his general encouragement expressed, in his standard farewell as you left his office, one which in later years as a supervisor of staff I occasionally employed, though not in George's Ian Paisley-like accent "keep up the good work, Geoffrey".

Chapter 10
Practical Caseload Management

The choice is that either you take control of your day, or it will control you.

*

A charity focusing on the needs of discharged prisoners began in 1924. It became the National Association for Discharged Prisoners Aid Society, commonly known from its acronym as NADPAS. Probation officers had previously only been involved with persons who were discharged from custodial settings like detention centres and approved schools on licence but, not with ordinary adult prisoners who, if they required help, could come to see our duty officer but many went to NADPAS. In 1967, and in order to accommodate the introduction of the parole system, the Probation Service was renamed the Probation and After-care service. So after 1967 the work of NADPAS was taken over by the probation service. In our office one of the volunteers from NADPAS, who happened to be a former police detective, was located in our office, and, together with one of the senior probation officers, formed a prison after-care 'unit'. They offered a service to prisoners who opted for some help upon discharge. They helped with accommodation issues, vocational issues and general counselling. A goodly number of prisoners availed themselves of this help. There were others who tried to abuse this offer.

At one point about this time, a prisoner was, on release, provided with money in cash as a discharge grant when they left prison. In effect it was one week's worth of Social Security money and meant that they did not have to rush straight from prison to the local Social Security office. Unfortunately, our nearest local prison was some 11 miles away, and, with a pub on virtually every corner, there was plenty of temptation for prisoners to celebrate their release before getting home. Not unusually the celebration was prolonged, and some men lost most, if not all, of their money. It was then the wont of many to decide to go and see the NADPAS charity man in the hope that he might give them some extra funds. They would not get any, but they were not to know that in advance.

Opposite the office was a railway yard boarded by a 5 foot high stone wall. Quite often the amount of alcohol taken led to the need for the use of a toilet, and it was not unusual to see three or four heads on the far side of the wall enjoying some relief. Interestingly, some 20 years or more later, they built a Crown Court on that site and the brickwork showed a white discharge which the builders said was lime from the mortar. I like to believe that it was more likely to be uric acid from the visitations of so many recently released intoxicated prisoners in years gone by.

Suitably relieved, they would enter the office to see George, the NADPAS man. His previous police training was invaluable, but his repartee was better. The drunks could be heard ascending the stairs towards the corridor which led to his office and he would come out of his door to await their arrival at the top of the stairs, at the further end of the corridor. When they appeared at the top of the steps and turned towards him he would yell "Stop!" With much giggling and effort they would come to a swaying halt.

"Keep your bloody heads up you lot, or you will spill some". George would say, "And if you are looking for money see this!"

Whereupon he would pull out his trouser pocket linings, he always kept his trouser pockets empty for this purpose. Without words therefore he indicated that another advance of money would not be forthcoming. I learnt a lot from George's techniques with drunks, and as they were the main substance misusers of the day, I had plenty on my caseload over the years.

*

George had his workload apparently well organised, would I ever manage with mine? Fortunately the importance of the diary had been part of teaching on the training course and no doubt it became a critical tool for me. I favoured a week to the view so that when seeking to make appointments the whole week was visible. The drawback was that the space for writing was limited. The Boots Scribbling Diary in a foolscap size was my main tool of caseload management for much of my career. On the left there were the appointments for the day and to the right the meetings that had actually taken place. It was then possible to use the latter as an *aide memoire* sometime later when I came to dictate entries for the "C" sheets of each case.

Pretty soon there developed a loose pattern. Monday morning was a day for catching up on arrests over the weekend and writing reports and then, in the afternoon, it was out on a number of home visits. Starting after lunch I would visit the unemployed or female clients who were at home with children, or matrimonial cases. This took us to school leaving time, when it would be visits to the younger clients and their parents. Finally between about 5-30 and 7 pm, those coming home from work. Whilst it is fair to say that I attempted to be home by 6 PM on a Thursday my wife, a child care officer, and I used to joke that we were rarely at home to hear the Archers on the radio 6:45 PM.

Tuesday was a morning for interviewing for social enquiry reports and then in the afternoon it was my main reporting session for office visits by clients on the caseload, and in the same sort of order of categories of client as described in the home visit arrangements as on Monday. This session ran from 2 pm to 7 pm and most usually would involve between 12 and 20 persons coming in to see me.

Wednesday was a day for prison visits in the morning and more home visiting in the afternoon. There was an attempt to finish at about 6-30 that day.

Thursday was primarily report interviewing and writing and hopefully an early finish.

Friday was general case administration and record-keeping. In addition report interviews and clients who could not manage other days in the week had to be fitted in, together with a further reporting session for workers who finished early on a Friday. So that meant that there was no early finish for me on a Friday

Then there was Saturday morning. Yes a 5 ½ day week in those days. Again those who could not get in during the week due to working away might be seen. Also periodically there was a need for one officer at court for the remand court. In those days courts in each area were required to sit locally on every day of the week except Sunday and Good Friday. So Saturdays and Bank holidays required staffing by our service.

This basic programme I have outlined was not fixed, apart from the prearranged home and office visits, and in between the other duties to be undertaken. Court duty I will discuss later, but also office duty. The service offered an instant access service to people with problems of any sort that might loosely relate to any of our broad responsibilities in the criminal or matrimonial areas of our work.

Very often there would be clients of colleagues who were out, and the client had an urgent problem. Unsurprisingly, this often involved a dearth of funds; and it probably meant that the client knew their own officer would give them nothing so they waited until they were out. Then there would be local drunks, not currently on supervision, also after money. To be fair some of the problems raised were genuine and often related to the failure to arrive of a giro cheque. In those cases we tried to help by phoning the Social Security office to plead the case put by the client. Sometimes, it became quickly clear that the client's version did not match the recorded facts. However, importantly you often found yourself representing people with genuine issues whose own ability to verbalise their personal case was lacking.

Interestingly, that was very akin to the role I felt we often ended up with in court work.

Together with the fact that there was a need to occasionally write reports at home (a court report was about two A4 pages of handwriting), I would judge that I and, most of my colleagues in those days, would often work 50 or more hours per week on average. Like many professionals of the day long hours were an accepted part of professional life. It is true that on one level it was exploitative, but, it was for most of us, an acceptable element of the great privilege of having control of your own work as befits the professional role. Twenty years or more later the 150 hours per four week contracts arrived, with requirements to complete timesheets and take time off in lieu when one exceeded one's hours. That, together with the redefining of clients to" offenders", and later "service users", denoted a move away from what we experienced in those halcyon days, of what felt like, independent professional status.

I must be careful with those rose tinted glasses, however. There were members of staff who took advantage of the lack of supervision and management. There were those who failed to keep the prescribed records; ironically some were very often hard-working officers who were administratively disorganised and attempted to justify their omissions by claiming it gave them more time to see clients.

However, a minority were lazy and / or were taking advantage, or in some cases ill-equipped for the job. Colleagues knew who they were, often through the simple expedient of having many of that officer's clients to be seen by the duty officer because the officer was out a lot; or worse seen in a bad light by the client. Also, they were the sort of officer whose reports were always late for court, or not done at all.

So I would accept that whilst the majority of officers took full responsibility for their own professional conduct, a minority did not. In an indirect way this minority provided an added excuse for the Home Office to insidiously allow the cult of managerialism to be introduced, and to lead to the gradual decline, of what I have described as, the individual independent professionalism of the probation officer role.

However, I had this caseload in one quadrant of the city, and I was doing all my new work in another. Before arriving to start work in the city I had only visited the place for my quasi interview, come appointment, experience. Learning the roads and routes was important, and I found a great deal of time could be saved by, wherever possible, planning visits in a logical route working out from the centre where the office was situated. Ideally, I would always arrange the last visit at the nearest point on the patch to home. I quickly learned that that in all aspects of the job, administrative planning was crucial. Managing a caseload well in excess of 80 was a norm in those days in our city. Having a good proportion of transferred cases was a help, since many were well into overall duration and were into some settled routine. Most probation orders were for two years and a significant number were for three. It took well into the 1970s to begin for us to begin to be successful in encouraging courts to make shorter orders. A probation order could be made for any period between one and three years, and the argument for shorter orders, eventually conceded by the courts, was that the most important work was done in the early part of the order.

As a rule of thumb in those days the client was seen weekly, or more often, in the first three months, then it might go out to fortnightly until a year, or the halfway point of the order, whichever came first, was reached. Then it could be not less than monthly. In exceptional cases where the client had made a big effort one could apply to the court for the order to be ended early for good progress.

Of course, any crisis and / or reoffending would usually mean a return to weekly contact. If you consider the model we were working to this all makes sense. An assessment set out the underlying issues likely to be responsible for offending. A plan to address these issues was made. The work to be done was embarked upon and it would be quickly clear whether or not the client was engaging, and if they were, it was turned into a monitoring and reminding operation. Any significant change like a breach of the order, or other significant problem issue like loss of accommodation would clearly nullify the present plan and a new one would be needed, and this was likely to need a return to more frequent contact, at least for a while.

So, we had probation orders of between a year and three years to supervise. Borstal licences of twelve months, detention centre licences of three months, and varying lengths of approved school after-care. Then, there were the orders, made by the family courts to supervise children in cases of marital breakdown. Starting in 1967 there were parole licences of varying length.

Given the numbers there were two basic principles that made for efficient case management. First there had to be personal organisation to ensure that you saw people in accordance with your plans, and second that you put a lot of effort into the first three months and then, in the average case, you moved from a proactive role to a monitoring role. This required a lot of discipline since many things got in the way of these principles, not least the inconvenient fact that some clients reoffended.

This begs an oft asked question as to what constituted success in working as a probation officer. Well over the years, the focus in probation, as in many other fields, such as education, has moved to the evaluation of outcomes. In many ways, in the age of post managerialism, this is understandable and indeed may be valid. On the other hand, I venture to suggest, that the view of myself and colleagues, in the heyday of probation workers, as I have called it, was that we were not statistical outcome driven, but quality of life driven.

If we could enable people to see that their lives might be improved by changing certain behaviour, and reducing their reoffending, then life for them and their family might indeed be better. This may, or may not, reduce offending immediately, although we strove to do that, but if clients learned a less antisocial way of living, it was likely to be both better for them, and coincidentally, society.

There we go again, social work principles to the fore. Enabling a client to become a better person was helpful to them first and society second. I felt very focused on my clients and their personal development. Obviously I wanted to stop them reoffending if I could, but that was a designed by-product of their understanding how to become a better and more socially acceptable person.

And did it work? I cannot answer that question in today's parlance of outcome statistics. Many academics will undoubtedly suggest that our work was not statistically successful, either in itself or in relation to the work with persons supervised on later orders which followed the death of the independent probation officer.

What I can say is that many of my clients did reoffend, as undoubtedly many service users of the present probation service do. I would expect that we offered life skills and challenges to behaviour which improved their lives and thereby probably reduced reoffending. I can also say that many people whom I expected to reoffended did not, and also in my 34 years in the same city I came across clients who expressed thanks for the interest shown in them and the guidance given to them by myself and my colleagues of the day.

Chapter 11
Engaging in the Clients' milieu

Milieu may be said to be a person's social environment.
*

There is an old joke; still amusing amongst my, now retired, friends and acquaintances, which goes like this:-
"He went to a good school."
"How do you know?"
"Because it was Approved."

It may not be funny to members of younger generations as they will be unaware that one of the often used sentences, for young people in the juvenile courts of the day, was that of making an Approved School Order. These orders which took children away from home could be made for social reasons, where the child was not being well cared for, or where the child was beyond the control of the parents. They could also be made for criminal offences that a child committed. These orders whisked children as young as 11 away from home to a residential boarding school. There was not one within 10 miles of our city, and a regularly used one was some 40 miles distant. The young person could be there for some time, coming home for school holidays. When they did leave they were on licence afterwards. Probation officers supervised those sent to approved schools for criminal reasons rather than social ones. These orders were abolished by the Children and Young Persons Act of 1969

"He will not get out of bed in the morning", said the mother of a young 15-year-old who was on approved school licence. Joseph was a typical teenager, hard to engage in any talking therapy process, and far better suited to practical action. The issue at the time was the need to get him into some employment or training, and an appointment had been arranged by me for him to pursue this.

It was a 0900 appointment in town and he lived about 3 miles distant. I realised that he would never make it without some intervention on my part. Mother was careworn, and had other children to deal with, and I forget but, dad either worked away or was not in the picture. So at 0815 on the appointed day, as agreed with his mum, I arrived at Joseph's house about 10 miles from my home. Mum informed me that even though he knew I was coming, and this was a big chance for him, Joe had still refused her calls to arise. I went upstairs to his bedroom in the three bedroomed semi-detached council house determined to get things moving.

What hit me were the conditions in with in which this young man had to exist. There were no carpets upstairs, just bare floorboards. In his room was a bed with a mattress, no sheets just coats piled on top of him. It was the early part of the year and a bitterly cold day and there was ice on the windows.....inside. I most certainly would have been reluctant to get out of bed in that house that day. It reminded me of the appalling circumstances in which some clients live, and why sometimes motivation to change could be so difficult to engender, in some cases, where their physical circumstances were dire.

*

So it was a task and a half to manage the demands of the caseload, and deliver the social work service to the individuals upon it. Organising oneself to ensure that people reported, and that you followed up those who did not, visiting the homes of those where that was part of the plan, and then recording the work. Most of all it was important to be organised to write the three monthly assessments or summaries as they were called. With over 80 cases that is getting on for about 30 a month. Looking back there is no wonder that some officers without administration abilities struggled. But aside from the caseload and court related work, there were contacts to be made with all sorts of agencies.

There were child care officers involved in some of the families where I also had somebody on supervision, and similarly families where mental welfare officers had a family involvement. It was crucial to get to know the staff involved and to be able to swap information about what we were doing. Quite often this was by informal contact out on "the patch" to which it was sometimes referred.

I can think of several roads on different estates where I would regularly visit three or more houses. Clients were aware of my red mini car and they also recognised the cars of the other social workers, so there was no point in trying to hide one's contact with another family. This interrelationship of families on estates was a large factor in offending. Very often the younger members of these, sometimes dysfunctional families, would work on offending ideas together, or egg one another on to do something illegal. Therefore it was only sensible to work with not just the individual client and his, for it was mainly lads, family, but also to work with two or three families whose offending children were interlinked. Because they recognised my car there was no point in attempting to deny that I was visiting another house across the road, so, far as was possible within the bounds of confidentiality one just worked with it.

Seeing the child care or mental welfare officers on the patch was also a bonus, and crucial in understanding what they were doing with members of the family with whom I was also involved. However, we all worked to casework rules of confidentiality and so there was a certain guardedness in what we said to one another, limiting it to the outline of work we were doing with our respective clients in the family. With the mental welfare officers, there was a much greater likelihood that in the overlap it was not just about family involvement, but about direct client involvement. Then, as now, there was a large amount of offending behaviour committed by people suffering from mental illness.

Looking back, I can see now that I was better able to understand the work of these colleague childcare and mental welfare officers because my training had involved me, even if only briefly, in their work. I had experienced the assessment of mentally ill patients, and I had been present when they persuaded clients to go voluntarily into hospital, and even taken them there when they were unwilling to go and had been sectioned under the then Mental Health legislation. I had seen the traumatic process of taking children into care, the obtaining of things like the FFI (freedom from infection certificate) and the rest. I also happened to be newly married to a child care officer and accompanied her when she was on evening or weekend call out (something my job did not require) to deal with emergencies.

These experiences gave me an understanding of the work of these people and therefore, I perhaps held them in more regard than did some of my own colleagues. Through no fault of their own, a number of my colleagues had no knowledge of the other agency workers' jobs, and its attendant pressures.

Matters were not helped with the publication of the Seebohm Report in 1968, which led, in about 1973, to the disbandment of these individual agencies and the creation of social services departments, where all staff were required to give up specialisation and take on a range of cases. One significant impact for the probation service was the arrival of some staff who did not want to work in the new setting, as they preferred to specialise, and on the other hand there were promotional opportunities in the new departments and we lost some staff the other way too. Was it a success? Well others will be better placed to judge, and sticking with my stated aim of not trying to comment on subsequent events, I will say simply this. It's unsurprising to me that after forcing staff to become generic in the 1970s there has been a slow drift back to specialism, most particularly in children's services and mental health.

Then there were the local police officers. In those days there was a clear view expressed by many police officers that we were do-gooders, or as a later comment, possibly first aired in the Reginald Perrin comedy television programmes of the 1970s, "namby-pamby probation officers". You have to remember that we were saying to our clients that we wanted them to be honest with us, as whatever they said was confidential. On the other hand, police intelligence was very much predicated upon police officers talking to informers and the public in order to build up pictures of those who had been, or were planning to be, involved in crime. We were therefore taught, that it was prudent not to divulge information to the police for fear that it would become obvious from the questioning, if a client was arrested, that we were the source of this and that it would ruin the trust of the offender with ourselves.

That is not to say that there was no line, such as might exist in the confessional, where we would withhold information about crime. I have countless times been with clients to the police station to hand themselves in. It would become obvious when a client was working up to tell you of something they had done wrong. At such points, I would always interject and remind them that whilst I was there to help them so far as I could, I could not condone offending and if you tell me something that means you have committed a crime, then I will have to take some action. Despite this warning most clients went on with their confession, because they wanted to unburden themselves, and really needed help to face up to the consequences.

That is not to say there were not grey areas. Social Security matters come to mind. A client may have just told me that he had secured a job after a period of unemployment and I might ask whether he had yet notified the Social Security office. The following silence spoke volumes; and was usually dealt with by an instruction from me to come and see me next week and to show proof that you have done something about informing them.

So, I hope I've shown that personal management and focus on the personal development of clients' lives were the main thrusts of the approach to individual supervision. And in order to further that, one needed to be out on the patch involved with those significant others involved in the client's lives and also with the other agencies, and their workers, who might also have an input to their lives, or that of their families.

If that had been all, the job as they say would have been a "good 'un". But a major interruption was the duty, second only in the 1949 probation rules to "advising assisting and befriending" clients; namely the responsibility to help the court by providing them with information to help them select the most suitable method of dealing with a case.

Chapter 12
The Probation Court Report
– to Enquire or to Inquire

"The court will wish to take into account all information as to the circumstances of the offence and the character of the offender, and, with this in view, paragraph 3 (5) of the Fifth Schedule (of the Criminal Justice Act 1948) provides that it shall be one of the duties of a probation officer to "inquire, in accordance with any directions of the court, into the circumstances or home surroundings of any person with a view to assisting the court in determining the most suitable method of dealing with his case".
Home Office Circular 220 / 1949. Criminal Justice Act 1948.
Summary Jurisdiction Rules

*

In the 1960s and 1970s the decision to prosecute was still with the police rather than the Crown Prosecution Service (CPS) which only arrived on the scene in 1985. Before then, in dealing with young offenders, in all but grave crimes, a police officer would report a juvenile offender aged under 18, in respect of the matters for which they had been apprehended. Indeed, in later years, these matters were referred to panels of police, social workers and probation representatives to consider whether prosecution was the best option, or if a formal caution issued by a senior police officer in uniform or some other diversionary process could be employed, to avoid a court appearance. Back then, in the years I am focussing upon, these panels did not exist. Sometimes weeks elapsed before a decision was taken between the point where the police officer took the child home, and told the parents that their offspring would be reported for the alleged matters, and further said that they would hear in due course. Police officers returning a child to their parents in such circumstances could genuinely say that it was not up to them to decide whether the case would go before a court or not, and perhaps sometimes it was easy to leave an impression that, hopefully, it may not.

The papers then went to a senior police officer who would have to make a decision based upon the nature of the crime and other factors such as the record, if any, of the young person concerned. Once a decision to prosecute had been made, and using a calendar of hearing dates provided by the court, the police selected a date some three or so weeks hence to then sent the details and the proposed date to the local court for them to prepare a summons to be sent to the child and his parents. Unfortunately the notice to prosecute that was sent to the courts was sent co-terminously to the probation office and it included a proposed date of hearing at juvenile court some three or so weeks hence.

Like many of us who wonder if we were just over the speed limit, when we went through a radar trap, we watch the post for a brown official envelope, and when one does not appear in a couple of weeks one hopes one was in fact driving within the speed limit. So it was for these young people and their parents. Hearing nothing for a few weeks meant they were probably okay.

Whilst the parents were in this state of hopefully avoiding a court appearance, we at probation had to get ourselves organised to make arrangements for preparing a report for the court which was expected in advance of the hearing in all juvenile cases unless there was to be a Not Guilty plea. In order to establish likely plea, and therefore know if a report would be required we needed an early contact with the parents. Preparing such a report involved interviewing the young person and their parents. Enquiries usually involved a home visit by the officer, followed by the youngster coming to the office subsequently and further enquiries, like contacting schools, or youth workers, or others. Therefore we often wrote immediately proposing a visit appointment. The courts, meanwhile, were often beset with work pressures and did not get round to preparing a summons for a few days after receiving the notice from the police, after all, from their viewpoint, the offenders could not object if they had a summons 7 to 10 days before court. So our letter was sometimes the first inkling the offender and his family received that the matter, which they hoped had gone away, most certainly had not.

And whom do surprised and upset persons hold responsible for their disappointment? Why, messengers of course.

So, often one would spend the first abortive half an hour of the visit to the home getting through the anger of parents disappointed that after all there was to be an official sanction. It got worse. Work pressures often meant one took a chance and out on the patch you took details of a report to be done on somebody whose street you would be passing and you thought you might call upon on 'spec'. Not a good idea. If they had the letter in advance they may still be angry with the messenger, but at least you were expected. Unexpected was not good.

A colleague and friend of many years, tells of the occasion in the 1970s, when he called unexpectedly at home in these latter, unannounced, circumstances. The father became so I irate that he armed himself threateningly with a hatchet. It took an hour of talking to defuse it all.

In later years this would no doubt have led to quite a kerfuffle. But, my colleague took the view, rightly in my opinion, that he could understand why the man was angry and even though his actions had gone too far there was in the end no harm done. He did not even charge for his extra underwear laundry bill. We all ensured thereafter that we sent advanced warning of visits.

*

There was, at that time, a debate about the nature of the work we did in relation to court reports. Did we,

Enquire - ask for information, investigate, look into, or did we

Inquire - which my dictionary, at least, suggests is another term for enquire.

At that stage there were probably 90 or so probation services in the country, all pretty autonomous. Some took the view that we should call our reports to the court, social enquiry reports "SER", others took the view they were social inquiry reports "SIR".

This argument may appear semantic, but it was a very real issue of the day. For many, me included, to enquire implied the social work ethic of getting alongside the client and engendering cooperation. But as time went on the more inquisitorial aspect of the word inquire made some staff feel that this was reflecting a tougher stance to rebut the "namby-pamby" epithets, to which I have already alluded. I experienced it as a real issue of principle, and was firmly in the SER camp.

Of course, how we got away with calling them SER for so long is surprising since the 1949 Probation Rules are quite clear that our duty was "*to inquire* in accordance with any directions of the court, into the circumstances or home surroundings of any person, with a view to assisting the court in determining the most suitable method of dealing with his case". (My italics)

Looking back, I wonder if one of the traits of officers of the probation heyday was a non-destructive anti-authoritarianism. The SER / SIR issue could have been a microcosm of that. You want us to be inquisitorial, we believe in enquiring. We were after all working with people, of whom many were unable to manage their own lives. Be this by dint of experiencing poor socialisation in their upbringing, or lacking in capacity to manage life in society, or who were slave to addiction. Of course those who were responsible for heinous crimes or who were, at that point unwilling to engage with us, we could not support, but for many who needed help to manage life, then we were really on their side and sometimes that meant helping them through the system.

In the reference to juvenile reports I mentioned the starting point was often at home and then little Johnny would come to the office to be seen solo, on a subsequent occasion. For the adults the reverse was the norm, and instead of a home visit a second office visit was sometimes more appropriate for single offenders living alone in bedsits. But these rules of thumb were not set in stone, and each case was dealt with on its merits. There would be a telephone contact with employers or any other source who could verify certain facts or build a picture of the offender, with the client's permission of course. On the rare occasion where permission to contact a third party was not forthcoming and you felt that this was a necessary contact, you still did not make that contact. But you did report to the court your reasons for wishing to make the contact and the fact that permission was refused, together with any stated reasons for this refusal. The court would then decide whether this was a relevant matter or not.

The format of the report began with basic details of the offender and his offence, and then there was usually a statement of the number of times the person had been seen, and where, and then reference to any other persons contacted or information obtained. In those days it was difficult to get any formal statement from the police about the circumstances of the offence and often the only information in that regard, that was readily available, was the offender's view. Clearly that was not helpful. That did change after the CPS came into being fifteen or more years later in 1985.

The whole process was inhibited where the person was not fluent in the language and an interpreter was needed. You quickly learned that there were good and bad interpreters. Some wanted to take the interview over and report what they wanted you to hear. Others could only operate by interpreting simple questions and answers. It was very difficult to get the "feel" of the client in such cases. Added to this was the fact that it was hard in those days to supervise offenders on orders where there was a language issue.

Did this mean that there was a disadvantage to these clients, in those days, if it was less likely for supervision to be proposed in our report? Yes, I suspect so. But as you may see shortly in relation to services available in different areas, the availability of options to courts was a geographic fact of life or should I say geographical lottery.

Moving on in the report; where there was a home visit there was usually a comment about the conditions of the home. I always wondered how I might have felt if my home environment had been assessed in a report. "Good", I could cope with, "adequate", would have been disappointing, and "poor" devastating. As a matter of interest "poor" usually reflected the fact that you wiped your feet when you came out. Here I may say that the housing stock of the day was often very poor. Many clients lived in what, today, would be considered sub-standard accommodation.

Next there was a social history, the social work model again. This would include reference to childhood, family, education and employment.

Then current circumstances, including the current living and working arrangements, and a fairly detailed breakdown of income and outgoings. This latter was primarily included to assist the court if they had to make a decision about fines or compensation.

Then there followed a comment about the offence, fairly short and bald in those days, and an assessment of the factors leading to that offending. Where the person had a previous record of offending that was also discussed, and comments about it made. Did the current offence fit into a pattern of previous offending? Was the present offence a sign that offending was escalating or de-escalating? If the person was of mature years, was there a lengthy gap since he last offended?

Finally, there was the conclusion, to which some sentencers were known to turn without bothering to look at the rest. This indicated the officer's opinion and sentencing options. It often referred to the likely impact of custody should that be imposed, and then went on to look at other options available to the court. It ended up with the officer's proposal for sentencing, especially giving the reasons for or against the use of probation supervision.

And what were the sentences of the 1960s? Moving through the hierarchy of sentences of the day looked something like this

There was, and still is, the absolute discharge, a sentence that is usually used to technically mark a finding of guilt but which the court does not feel requires direct punishment.

The conditional discharge, as I have described earlier, was a very good sentence and was effectively the probation order without supervision. Its duration could be anything between one and three years. Incidentally, I believe that some extra conditions were permissible, and I seem to think that in those days Channel Islands courts made conditional discharges including a condition that required the offender not to return to that island for the duration of the period specified. Not an option for our city magistrates; although I'm sure they would have welcomed it.

The fine was popular because of the vast swathe of motoring cases which filled court lists of the day. Indeed, this was the most frequent penalty imposed by magistrates' courts. Also as indicated at the very start absolute destitution was rare and there was now a provision for social security payments, so virtually everyone therefore had an income, however meagre, from which at least weekly payments could be made.

Then, of course, the probation order, which I will discuss in more detail a little later.

It should be noted that it was not until after 1973 that Community Service Orders (CSO) appeared. They were, and are, under their more recent embodiment as community payback or unpaid work orders, very popular. In the simplistic ideas of the time, probation was directed towards reform whilst CSO's were clearly retributive and courts were easily able to grasp the difference, and to tailor their sentencing accordingly. If they could, in those years, have made the combination of requirements, such as were later available, then I am sure the courts would have used them together. But I like to think that in those days the lack of that combined facility made the need to choose one principle over another resulted in a much clearer focus in sentencing.

There was the detention centre for the under 21s. The much vaunted "short sharp shock" of between three and six months followed by a short licence period under the supervision of a probation officer. During the 1970s its virtues were extolled as being of use for first offenders committing violence offences and also for football hooligans. I believe the experiment was a complete failure and many young men, who might never have experienced custody, did so, and their record reflects it still. Detention Centres too disappeared by 1991.

From 1967 there was the suspended sentence of imprisonment. In its first guise, which was during the period I'm concentrating upon, it was misused both by courts and probation colleagues; for different reasons. Courts, who should instead of sending people to prison for what they had done, or alternatively making a probation order, chose the sort of middle course of the suspended sentence. And, I am sad to say, that a few of my colleagues of the day were far too keen on proposing suspended sentences, often inappropriately. At the time my colleagues had heavy caseloads and were writing up to 10 court reports per month. By the late 1980s it was felt that a court report was a full day's work when adding up interview and other enquiries and preparation time, together with the writing thereof. In the 1960s we did not have time management and some reports did take that sort of time allocation, but the experienced officer had to cut corners or else, as my wife reminds me, write reports in the evenings and at weekends at home, because we did. Add this to the caseload pressures already mentioned, and for some officers the only way to keep down caseload numbers was to not propose probation orders, because, in our city, if you proposed it and one was made, you got the case.

This led to proposals for suspended sentences in cases which really did not justify that course. The officer under caseload pressure, or dealing again with a client they had worked unsuccessfully with before, or a client who maybe was a pain, went for the "bender" as the suspended sentence was colloquially known. This reporting officer 'new case deflection' technique may not always have been conscious, but it compounded the keenness of the courts to use this sentence. They, of course, felt it showed the public that they were "macho" and they were sending people to prison. That was the local newspaper headline; only defendants were not actually going to jail. It looked better in the press than, say, a probation order. Where I will give the courts of the day their due however, is that they did often activate the suspended sentence if the offender committed new offences in the period of suspension. The trouble was that they, of their own volition, and sadly with the unintended collusion of some probation officers, passed the sentences inappropriately in the first place, in too many low level cases. They then lost the initiative when the person reoffended and sent them to jail. This sort of thinking and action contributed significantly to the burgeoning prison population of the 1980's.

In turn this led to the very laudable philosophy espoused in the 1991 Criminal Justice Act. This postulated that for anything other than the least serious offences, courts must judge whether the offence was 'so serious' as to require immediate imprisonment, or else, that it was 'serious enough' to warrant a community penalty. In this clearly logical thinking there was no room for a suspended sentence. However, the law was wise enough to concede that in all human life there are exceptional cases. So it permitted the use of the suspended sentence in "exceptional cases", which case law then determined was very exceptional indeed. For example, a person suffering a terminal illness might be given one. During the whole of its period of several years of operation that version of the suspended sentence was very sparingly used.

I promised at the outset to keep within the bounds of what I have described as the heyday for the independent professional probation officer ending in 1991, when the probation order was killed off by that very same Criminal Justice Act. But following my above theme on the use of suspended sentences, I must make this exception in briefly commenting upon later developments. As appreciative as I am of the new approach to suspended sentences from 1991 onwards, I was appalled that the judiciary pressurised Parliament to reverse the logic of the 1991 Act in 2003 and to open up the use of the suspended sentence again. Courts, in my experience, love that "macho" sentencing which I described earlier and so the use of the suspended sentence has again risen – and so, unsurprisingly, repeating history, has the prison population.

I return to the available sentences of the 1960s, and moving up to sentences which could only be imposed at either the Quarter Sessions or Assizes. There was Borstal training for young men. In the early years of the 1900s, at the same time as the idea of probation was being formed, Mr Evelyn Ruggles-Brise, fresh back from learning about the treatment of young offenders in America, started the Borstal system; named after the Kent village where the first institution was located. The underlying idea was to take serious young offenders, for one or two years, and train them in skills like bricklaying and carpentry. On release, they would be on licence to a probation officer for a year and subject to recall for not keeping its terms. At the outset, Borstal trainees were specially chosen from the then population of young offenders. Unsurprisingly, they picked the best and the early reconviction rates, after two years from release, were as low as 20%. By the time I was supervising Borstal licences, and all young people sent to Borstal went through a now universal system, the reconviction rate was up to 80%. Unsurprisingly the sentence disappeared in 1982 and was replaced by Youth Custody.

Also, from memory, Borstal licensees wore the "Borstal spot", done in Indian ink, on the cheek bone. This tattoo became a lot less common after the abolition of Borstal. Prison tattooing was very prevalent in those days, for example a common prison tattoo is four dots or the letters ACAB tattooed across the knuckles of the criminal which stands for "all coppers are bastards". Or a dot on each hand, in between the thumb and forefinger, one meaning one going into prison and one meaning they have completed their sentence. A spider web usually symbolised a long sentence prisoner.

For those over 21 there was imprisonment. Over the years, and in discussion with sentencers, I have responded to the accusation that probation reports never proposed custody, by pointing out many cases where we have. It is fair to say that in my early days we offered options in case the court felt that, after hearing mitigation on the day, they would not use custody. Ironically, I clearly remember having to deal with a number of cases where the report said custody, and the court wanted something else.

So, it was this broad set of options that the officer needed to consider in giving their opinion to the court. Taking into account any specific disposal, suggested by the court, the officer tried to match what they discovered in their enquiries, to the "most suitable" disposal for the court to consider. This would often be reached by elimination of the less suitable sentences for the particular offender.

The actual report writing was done by the individual officer, whose background in the English language was variable. I suppose my generation were brought up reading books, and you learned, as well as being taught in school, about grammatical construction. But officers in my city were, I'm sure quite typical, some were good report writers and others less so. We had former army and police officers who tended to be formalistic and stilted in their presentation, by dint of the sort of reports they'd had to write in their previous working lives. We had graduates, used to waxing lyrical in essays and other academic forums (or is that 'fora?'). We had those with no formal writing training whose style was more like letter writing. Finally there were officers for whom reports were of special interest and amongst them I would like to number myself.

For some, the PSR was an art form in itself. We believed in making the report hang together logically, leading to a conclusion, which should be quite expected by the reader when he or she reached it. This logic was also to be presented in a readable form. I referred earlier to complaints from my good lady about writing reports in the evenings and weekends. It was wrong of me, and I fully accept that. However, I experienced PSR writing as a really interesting part of my work, and enjoyed the task so, that, in retrospect, I fully justify my misdemeanour, by saying that, the act of writing them was part of my work but it was also a bit of a hobby as well.

I was often impressed by the quality of some of the PSR's going to court which passed through my hands, though some were very ordinary, and a good few dire. My long-term colleague Mike, whose reports were consistently excellent, and were often complimented upon in court, had a lively tongue in cheek approach to them. I asked him once about the meaning of a word that was totally unfamiliar to me, in his report; he was delighted and said that he was so pleased because if I didn't understand it then neither would the court. "Always try to put an obscure word into my reports to keep the buggers on the bench on their toes"

My best effort at obfuscation was in a SER to the quarter sessions and concerned a security guard who had facilitated the burglary of a factory. I managed to get in the phrase "*quiz custodiet ipsos custodies*". I thought that referring to the Latin phrase for "who will guard the guards" was quite smart. But then as a friend reminds me "nobody likes a smartarse"

However Mike's superior abilities are summed up by this wonderful turn of phrase which speaks for itself, it came in a case of a first time offender convicted of theft. Just remember that our city was at least 50 miles from the nearest bit of sea.

"After 13 years in the Royal Navy Smith has found his return to civilian life not to be an easy experience, particularly in terms of gaining employment. He had been a deep sea diver, and there is not much call for that particular skill in our city".

(For some more of these "Slips of the report writers pen" as I will call them I refer the reader to Appendix 2)

Chapter 13
The Probation Order of the 1960s

"3.-(1) Where a court by or before which a person is convicted of an offence (not being an offence the sentence for which is fixed by law) is of opinion that having regard to the circumstances, including the nature of the offence and the character of the offender, it is expedient to do so, the court may, instead of sentencing him, make a probation order, that is to say, an order requiring him to be under the supervision of a probation officer for a period to be specified in the order of not less than one year nor more than three years"
Criminal Justice Act 1948

*

Later in my career I was given the responsibility of addressing all new magistrates in our county about the role, function and practice of the probation service locally. Sometimes, after I had delivered my session to a group of new magistrates, it was possible for me to join them informally for coffee or lunch, depending on the timing of the end of my session.

On one occasion in the 1980s I was intrigued by a discussion that was going on between two new magistrates in respect of sentencing issues. A major trunk road passed through the whole of our county. One petty session's area held jurisdiction over the southern half of this road and another petty sessions area held responsibility for the northern part thereof. The new magistrates had already experienced sitting in court with more experienced members of their bench and so had some experience of the sentencing "norms" in their area. The question arose as to the likely punishment to be meted out to a well remunerated company director, with no prior convictions, stopped by the police for travelling at 100 mph on a road whose speed limit was 70 mph.

In one court, it was reported that the general approach would be to impose a short three month immediate driving ban on the person, together with a modest financial penalty. The standard view of the other bench would be that whilst points were put onto the person's licence, and a swingeing fine imposed, there would be no immediate ban.

So depending upon whether you were caught one side of the dividing line or the other, your sentence could be significantly different. All perfectly legal; but all perfectly incongruous.

Justice, in the days when the probation order still existed, was still parochial, governed only by the statutory maxima prescribed by the relevant Acts of Parliament with the occasional nod to Case Law.

*

The general outlines of a probation order have already been set out, but it is worthwhile looking at the practicalities in a little more detail. First of all it is worth saying that the address at which the offender lived, or was intending to live after the court hearing, was quite significant. The role of supervising the order, in a legal sense, was allocated to the magistrates or petty session's area court in which that address was situated, they became the 'supervising court'. In effect they took on the legal management of the order, and were able to make alterations to the conditions where they were needed. A magistrates' court order, whether or not made in their local area to start with, could be dealt with by the supervising court, including the fact that they had power to revoke the order and to deal with the original offence.

When an offender changed address to a different area then there was the need to transfer the order and this was done by contacting the local probation office covering the new address and after they had established contact you would prepare papers to put before the court effectively substituting in the order the name of the new supervising court for your local court. Failure to invoke this procedure could cause enormous problems particularly if you needed to try to get the offender back before the court and the place they had moved to was a long way away.

Where an order was made at a quarter sessions or assize court, the order would specify the supervising magistrates' court. That magistrates' court could then make necessary amendments to the order and even deal with a breach of its condition. But they did not have the power to sentence for the original offence. Where they found that the order had been breached, and additionally felt that the order should be revoked, then they were required to send that order back to the higher court which had made it and they would either bail the offender to appear there or in some circumstances he would be sent in custody.

Earlier I have rehearsed the issue of the need for the offender to consent to the order. Before making an order the court was required to 'explain to the offender in ordinary language' the effects of the probation order and of all the requirements to be inserted in it, and that, if they failed to comply with any of them, or committed another offence, they would be liable to be sentenced for the original offence. Upon the making of a new order there was an expectation of the court that the offender would be seen quickly. In the Summary Jurisdiction Rules of 1949 it says *"it is important to establish as soon as possible a personal relationship between the probation officer and the probationer, and the court will no doubt think it desirable whenever practicable to arrange that, before the probationer leave the court, he shall see the probation officer who will supervise him or at least be informed of his name"*.

The order itself usually contained three basic conditions.

The first was that the probationer should keep in touch with the probation officer in accordance with such instructions as may from time to time be given, and in particular that they should allow visits to their home. This was the basic reporting condition that established the contact requirements in an order. The actual location, frequency and timing of meetings were then a matter for the officer and client. One thing that was felt important was that any meetings should not interfere with the client's employment. This in turn had implications for the officers who would have to see workers outside their employment hours.

The second general provision was that the probationer should inform the probation officer immediately of any change of residence or employment. A requirement designed to establish that we knew where the offender was living and working.

The third provision was that the probationer should be of good behaviour, which was generally aimed at the issue of re-offending, but it also gave us a loophole to act in terms of breach if the client was being unruly or disruptive in the interview or office.

In addition to these three basic conditions it was possible to add others.

Of those regularly used, an additional condition specifying place of residence was significant. This permitted the court to require the offender to live at a particular address, occasionally this was a private address with, say relatives, but more often it was used to require the offender to live in a probation hostel where the staff would help him to deal with the issues behind his offending.

My own experience with the use of hostels was, to say the least, mixed. I do recall one younger member of a group of five siblings who were very prone to offending, successfully being made subject of an order to reside in a hostel in another part of the country. This had the effect of getting him away from very negative local influences and he went on to gain employment and to set up home in that new area, and so far as I know, to lead a successful if not crime free life there.

On the other hand, I once conveyed a young man from our Quarter Sessions to a hostel some distance away from his home. He had fully agreed with me, whilst in custody on remand, that his best chance of avoiding custody was to move away from the group of young men with whom he was offending in his home area. He therefore agreed to attend this particular hostel and, as required in those days, I transported him in my mini car the 120 miles involved. I then left him in the care of the hostel staff and as it was late in the day, I went for a meal before driving home. As far as I can understand it he probably passed me on the drive home, in a car which he had stolen, and arrived back in in our home city before me.

Another regularly used additional condition related to the issue of mental health. I have no doubt that the link between mental health and offending has existed from time immemorial, and so it was only right that there was an option to refer people to the psychiatric services for assessment before a probation order was made. If a psychiatrist reported to the court that the offender was suffering from a mental illness then there were two options. An order could be made requiring them to be an inpatient in a mental hospital, but more usually the order was for them to receive outpatient treatment from a psychiatrist. This sometimes led to interesting professional differences of opinion. A psychiatrist might tolerate missed appointments as part of their treatment plan more readily than probation officers, who were supposed to monitor that clients attended for treatment. If the psychiatrist would not say that the offender was missing the appointments then the officer would have difficulty in proving that the offender was in breach of their order. There was not usually a problem with the slowly increasing number of forensic psychiatrists, who knew about the rules on reporting and also knew that the court would be unhappy if they did not ensure that the probation officer was kept up to date with all practical issues in the case. It was a problem with the occasional community psychiatrist who was only interested in his patient's illness and felt limited obligation to a probation officer or court.

As time went by other local methods of dealing with offenders were developed in different parts of the country. I have already indicated that local probation committees were in those days very much in charge of their local probation service and were sometimes persuaded to support some good ideas which local officers had devised. An example of these local initiatives in our area were motor education projects dealing with offenders who were convicted of offences such as TWOC (taking a vehicle without the owner's consent) and DWD (driving whilst disqualified) offences, and who did not need the full casework treatment (despite the Freudian concept that some driving offences could be related to sexual issues!), but who might benefit from education about driving related matters. Later on other mini courses were devised by probation officers in different areas for things like domestic violence and sex offending.

This led to what I used to call the CCC or Carlisle, Coventry and Croydon sentencing effect. By this I meant, that it depended where you were sentenced, as to what might be available. So for example in our city we may have had a motor education project but not a sex offender's project. A sex offender, therefore who fell to be sentenced for an offence in another area, and who might, had they lived in that area, been referred to their sex offenders group, could not be referred to ours, because we did not have one.

If you take the example of the 100mph driver referred to in the anecdote at the start of this chapter together with the CCC effect I have just outlined it will be evident that sentencing decisions could be constrained by both availability of provisions and local bench policies

A slight digression is needed here to expand on the issue of different provisions being available in different areas. It returns us to the role and structure of the probation services of the day. I have already discussed the independence of role of the probation officer in those days, together with the light touch of management. At that time centre did not, by and large, come up with new with ideas and promulgate them downwards. Instead, individual professional staff identified issues which might be dealt with in an alternative manner to that of normal one to one supervision. An individual, or small group of officers, would then devise a scheme which they would run with the cooperation of other office colleagues, who allowed them the time to do this work by themselves covering for the absence of the staff involved. The local magistrates were kept informed via the medium of the probation committee. Once a new model had been devised and tested and found to be useful, the details were then shared with colleagues in other areas. One of the most effective methods of this sharing came through the National Association of Probation Officers (NAPO) which, in those days, was a significant vehicle for discussing and sharing professional issues, later, with the onset of managerialism it was forced into much more of a trade union role.

Finally, there was a catchall which was rarely used and was under the general provision that a specific extra condition could be imposed, if it was felt appropriate in order to secure the good conduct of the offender. It was not often employed, but I did deal with one interesting case where it was most appropriate.

A young woman had worked in an accounts department and had misused her position in order to steal about £1500 from her employer. As a result, and despite being a first time offender, but because she had breached a position of trust, she received a custodial sentence, during this time she gave birth to a daughter. On release from prison, and being over 21, she was not subject to any statutory supervision and she did not avail herself of voluntary after care. Her relationship with her partner broke down and she was left a single parent. Some three years after her original offence, and under significant financial pressure, she obtained employment in the finance office of another company. She had gained this employment by failing to disclose her previous offending. She went on to steal another sum in excess of £1000 and her case went again to the Quarter Sessions. In my report I suggested to the judge that despite, as a first offender being sent to prison, she had reoffended in an almost copycat manner.

Her circumstances were now different, because she had the sole care of a 3 year old child and there was a significant chance that the child may have to go into the care of the local authority, were she to be imprisoned. I argued that her original custodial sentence had not deterred her from a similar repeat offence and that whilst prison was clearly justified, she would undoubtedly loose her home, and her child would have to be cared for at public expense. On the other hand there was no sign of her having a tendency to commit other types of crime and, therefore, if we could keep her away from work where she handled money, that may have the effect of preventing further offending.

My proposal was that a probation order might be made with an additional condition. The condition suggested was that she not undertake any paid employment without the **prior approval** of the probation officer. This I argued would deter her from trying to get a job where money was involved because she had to tell me before taking any job, and if she did not then she was liable to be brought back to court for breach of the order. The court felt that it was an appropriate condition and made an order in those terms. I supervised her for the following three years, she worked part time with my approval in a local factory, a job she obtained with the employers being aware of her offending and she committed no further offences. So far as I am aware did she not appear before the courts again.

Once upon a time, I was asked by a magistrate what the most effective way of making a probation order was. My response was to say that where I had connected with the client during the writing of the report, gone through the report with them and enabled them to understand the purpose of the order, and the work that I felt needed to be done, that we were partway there. Then, if I could be at court, that would be a bonus, and in addition if the magistrate making the order could look away from the prepared script on the bench, and look the defendant in the eye as they enunciated the conditions, that too made a big difference, because in my experience clients did most definitely take to heart the formal words spoken in court. Finally, if that magistrate could say to the defendant that I was in court and that he expected the defendant to see me straight after the hearing that was, in my view, a confirmation of the tripartite contract that was, the essence of the probation order.

Chapter 14
Breach of Probation Order

"If the probationer fails to comply with any requirement of the order, the procedure for dealing with him is that prescribed by section 6: if he is convicted of another offence committed during the probation period, he can be dealt with for the original offence under section 8."
Criminal Justice Act 1948. Summary Jurisdiction Rules 1949

*

Part of doing court duty required that, when a colleague could not be present in court in person to present their report, then you, as duty officer did so, on their behalf. In our court, in those days, you were required to provide a copy of the report for each of the magistrates, normally three, one for the clerk of the court and one for the solicitor for the defence, although this latter was usually provided to them in advance of the case being called on. When it was, and after the prosecution had reminded the bench of the facts of the case, if it was your report then one went into the witness box and took the oath, or affirmation, following it with one's name and job title and usually with some comment along the lines "this is my report Your Worships, I would invite you to read it, and I will be happy to answer any questions which you may have".

Incidentally, in adjourning for reports the court indicated whether or not they would be "part heard"; in other words the same bench would hear the case next time, if it was not then the case came before a new set of magistrates. We also had a system where the magistrates gave the clerk of the court an indication of what they saw as the issues they most wanted to hear about and also any sentence they had in mind. This was an informal notice to us and was not binding.

When acting as court duty officer, where you knew a colleague would not be able to attend, it was good practice, to read through their report before you went to court in order to be familiar with its contents and therefore able to answer any simple questions that the court might have about it. On this particular day I had not had chance to read the report as it was in a court that I was not due to cover. Partway through the session my other court colleague was called away, and in her absence, the report case was called on before the court she was covering. I hurried along and arrived in time to put in the reports to the magistrates. I then retired to the probation seat to take stock of the situation.

In the dock was a fairly care worn young woman, who, according to the report before me, had been convicted for loitering for the purposes of prostitution. As years went by the probation service had less and less to do with what came to be termed low-level matters, of which loitering for the purposes of prostitution was one. Back then however, courts were very concerned, especially about very young women, who were convicted of prostitution and hoped that they could be "saved" by the intervention of probation officers. So it was that we wrote quite a few reports about prostitutes with a view to determining whether or not they could be assisted to leave that occupation. In some ways it had echoes of our involvement in the rescuing of drunks in those days around the inception of the probation order.

The young woman concerned was visible only from the waist up, because the dock rail and wooden panel below it concealed her lower half. Being a man of the world, it was possible for me to determine the following. That the tee shirt she wore was indeed the only item of apparel covering her from her navel upwards. The tee shirt itself was straining to contain the upper forward part of her torso.

I thought I had better at least look through the report of my colleague to see what was being proposed. There was a lot of information which painted a picture of a young woman who had been encouraged into prostitution because of fairly dire personal circumstances. However, with, perhaps, an unfortunate turn of phrase, my colleague ended her report thus………..……….."In view of the circumstances I have outlined, I would propose to the court, that consideration be given to the making of a probation order in this case, as Miss Jones is clearly in need of some support."

Well…………….. everyone in court could see that.

The way I liked to look at the process of breach, as it was practised in those days, needs reference back to my contention that the probation order was a contract, between the court and the defendant and the probation officer was third-party to that contract with the role of ensuring the client's adherence to the conditions. So, where the conditions were not met, or in other parlance the rules were breached, it was necessary for the probation officer to make a complaint that, in his or her view, the offender had failed to comply with one or more of the conditions. Whatever the probation officer thought, was, on one level immaterial, because the court would need to decide whether their order had in fact been breached or not. Indeed the officer had to prove their allegation of breach "to the satisfaction of the court".

The process in those days was cumbersome and lengthy. First of all you needed to make your complaint and this was done by the preparation of an 'Information', a legal document setting out the terms of the original order and the allegation of the way in which the probationer was alleged to have failed to comply with it. The Information was then typed up at the probation office and taken before a justice of the peace who would decide whether or not there was a *prime facie* case made out. If the magistrate found that there was, then a summons could be issued to bring the probationer before the court. In a case where the whereabouts of the offender were unknown, or in other exceptional circumstances, application could additionally be made, by the officer on oath, for a warrant of arrest. If we were proceeding down the summons route, the Information would then go into the court office who would retype the details from it into a summons and send it to the probationer. The whole process was therefore quite lengthy, and it might take six or seven weeks from the date of the alleged breach of the order, to the matter coming before court.

As time went by the speed of this process was vastly improved. Firstly, by probation services undertaking to prepare summonses as well as the Information and this saved court processing time, and subsequently by them being able to set court dates themselves within a relatively short period of time. But the old system did have some uses. The lapse period between the breach and the court hearing provided the officer with an opportunity to encourage the probationer, in cases of alleged missed appointments, to attend on several occasions on the basis that this could be reported when the probationer appeared in court and thereby stand them in good stead. On the downside a probationer who did not cooperate in that interim period got away with six or seven weeks of non-attendance.

For the vast majority of probationers facing alleged breach at a court hearing, the outcome was likely to be that the order would be allowed to continue and that they would be given an admonishment, or at worst, be required to pay a small fine. It was only where there was an early and flagrant breach or where the probationer had been breached on several occasions that you got to the point of the order being revoked, and them being resentenced for the original offence.

It is fair to say that the independent professional probation officer of the day probably had their own view about the usefulness, or otherwise, of the breach process. I know that I took the view that it was a very useful tool in trying to ensure that the probationer engaged with you. During my first or a very early interview with a new probationer I would go through a copy of the court order with the client and get them to endorse the back of the order to say that they had received a copy of it and they understood it as its terms had been explained to them by me. Additionally I would in less formal terms say something along the lines of, "you must stick to these requirements to keep your appointments and contact me either in advance if you are likely to miss any appointment, alternatively contact me as soon as possible afterwards, if you are unable to contact me before. If I have to come chasing after you I will not be a happy man and I will have no compunction in taking you back to court".

Given that I had said that, I felt it only right to follow through in those cases where people did not comply. Now there was no way of comparing my stance on breach with that of others, however after the 1974 local government reorganisation when the number of probation services was vastly cut, my city was absorbed into a much larger probation area. They then financed a research department. Shortly after this, I was informed that in an analysis of completed cases where breach had been instigated, then 7.3% of my cases had been breached by me, which was apparently the highest percentage in the sample.

The role of the probation officer in the breach process was an interesting one. Firstly, there was the relationship with your client who may turn up on the day wondering what was going to happen, unless they had been reporting in the interim in which case they were already aware of my position. My stance in cases was to approach clients before court and tell, or remind, them what I was proposing to do if they pleaded guilty to the breaches which I had alleged. As indicated, in the vast majority of cases I was going to be seeking a slap on the wrist and ask the court to allow the order to continue. In those cases virtually everyone was happy to plead guilty and get the matter over with. Where however, my view was that the order should be revoked, and another sentence put in its place, there was a greater likelihood of a not guilty plea. Although to be fair back then not guilty pleas were far less common than in later years.

The next peculiar aspect was that when you went to court, and if the probationer pleaded guilty, you were responsible for telling the court the 'case for the prosecution', as it were. So when had they missed appointments, or what else had they done to breach their order. Once you had told the magistrates that, you took off the 'prosecution hat' and put on the 'independent probation officer' one. Under this second guise, you told the court how the order had gone overall and why, as this was usually the case, the order should continue. Finally, if the order was allowed to continue you took the probationer outside and gave him his reporting instructions for the next meeting.

As indicated by the quotation at the beginning of this chapter there were two forms of breach. Under Section 6 of the Criminal Justice Act 1948 and re-enacted by the same numbered section of the Powers of Criminal Courts Act 1973 whose provisions amended some aspects of probation law in the 1948 Act, action could be taken against people who breached the rules of the order by failing to report, notify a change of address, or otherwise failed to comply with their conditions. The other form of breach was dealt with under Section 8 of those Acts and was where a probationer committed a further offence during the currency of a probation order. You may wonder how it could come about that somebody could commit a further offence, and their original probation order would not be dealt with by the court hearing the new matter. Well to start with we go back to the issue of the supervising court; and if a probationer committed offence in another area then, that other court may not have had the power to deal with the order. Also those days preceded the 'electronic age' and the updating of police previous conviction lists was neither as timely, as in later years, nor as easily accessed, especially if you were apprehended in a new area far from your own home.

The vast majority of breach cases were dealt with on first hearing and within six or seven weeks of the alleged infringement. The bonus of this was that you were up to speed with the matters because they were fresh in your mind. Those cases that produced the problem in presenting them to the court, were matters where a warrant had been issued in order to get the offender before the court.

Warrants for breach came about in one of two ways. Firstly, as indicated, the offender had moved from their home and you did not have an address for them, therefore a summons couldn't be sent and so a warrant was issued. The second sort of case, and the most common, was where the summons was issued to an address where you believed the probationer to be living, and then they failed to show up to answer that summons. It was practice in such cases to seek a warrant without bail. The problem here was that it might take quite some time before the offender was apprehended, mostly when they had committed a new offence. In some cases this period was extensive and did lead to problems if our records were not very good or even not available.

Earlier, I did mention that I always tried to fully observe the law, and so must now, somewhat ruefully, admit a misdemeanour on my part in relation to a probation warrant. I was on office duty in about 1969. A woman in her thirties came in and was clearly very nervous before explaining that she thought she was in trouble, and wondered if I could help her. In 1956, as a teenager, she had been made subject of a probation order. It appears that her offence of theft related to her experience of a very unhappy home life. It was this factor which led to the officer proposing the probation order. For some months she complied fully and the officer noted the severe difficulties at home that this young woman was experiencing. Then suddenly aged about 19, she left home; effectively she ran away. The parents reported to my former colleague the fact that she had disappeared and told her that she had gone to stay with a friend in London; the parents were happy to see her go and were not going to pursue her. Because there was no forwarding address a warrant was issued, and had remained outstanding for some 11 years, at that point the woman appeared in my office. She told me that she was now happily married with children; her husband was in employment but had taken time off work so that she could come back to her home city and sort out the trouble she believed herself to be in, for skipping her probation order. Technically I should have taken her straight to the police station. Instead I took full particulars, including her current home address in London, explained what I was going to do, and told her that I was trusting her to meet me at court the following morning. She went off to stay overnight with an aunt, evidence of whose address she had also provided me with.

The enquiries I made of the police warrant office confirmed to me that, so far as records showed, her only offence was the one for which she was subject of the probation order, there had been nothing since. She did indeed meet me at the magistrates' court the following day where I had arranged for the warrant to be produced. I did explain to the magistrates that we had a very brief record of her contact with us. However, given that she stayed out of trouble for 11 years and had voluntarily surrendered herself, I was hoping that they would take a lenient view and take no further action in relation to the breach, which would mean that as the order was now ended she would free be free to go home. The court felt that this was a sensible course of action and made an order accordingly.

My independent professional commitment to the tripartite contract between court, client and me led, as I have shown, to a high level of breach cases being instigated by myself. Why then did some colleagues use this tool more sparingly? Perhaps their clients were more compliant than mine. Perhaps they were better at engaging clients than I. But one potential other explanation maybe that instigating breach was to voluntarily add more work to an already busy job. First there was the administrative aspect and secondly the need to be available to present the case when it came up in court.

For me the use of the court was critical in holding the clients to account on the one hand, and on the other to ensuring that the courts were confident in the knowledge that their orders were being well managed. As an unintended by-product my profile in the local courts was raised because as well as doing court duty in my turn, and going along with my social enquiry reports I was also there presenting my breaches.

Chapter 15
Courts – A market place

"The market-place, the eager love of gain,
Whose aim is vanity, and whose end is pain!"
Morituri Salutamus:
Poem for the Fiftieth Anniversary of the Class of 1825 in Bowdoin College
Henry Wadsworth Longfellow

*

In 1974 our son Alistair was born. There was all the excitement and anxiety of dealing with one's first born. After a few days off work I returned there, to the congratulations of many colleagues and genuine pleasure expressed by those members of the court fraternity with whom I came into contact.

Thirty four days later that same year, I returned home for tea, and baby, who had been progressing normally and well, was asleep upstairs. Sometime later my wife went to check on him and shouted to tell me that he was in severe distress. It was clear that there was a need for immediate medical attention. She grabbed him and we flew out and into the car and drove to the city hospital, which was some 5 miles from our house. We made it in less than 10 minutes, and I know that I went through at least a couple of red lights and drove in excess of the speed limit. We ran into A & E and basically shouted help. The medical staff were instantly responsive, and did their best. He died of causes that were never really fully explained.

Upon my return to work I received a considerable amount of sympathy and support, again not just from colleagues, where one might have expected it, but also from the wider court fraternity. People, whom I did not know very well, expressed their shock and sympathy in a very positive way towards me. A number of magistrates, some of whom I only knew by sight, wrote to me, and several of them subsequently invited myself and my wife to meet with them socially.

One of the court reporters for the local newspaper, with whom I had previously only exchanged pleasantries, approached me, and in due course I got to know that his daughter had died, aged about five, with cystic fibrosis. He and his wife, together with me and mine, met socially and became friends; we still are.

Courts are about arguing the law in respect of cases. But the argument is about the law and not about the people who put the arguments. My experience of personal tragedy was also an experience of the strength of spirit amongst those who ply their trade in a local court setting.

*

In one sense you could see courts as a market place; different players coming to one point to do business. Undoubtedly, deals were done between defendants and their representatives and prosecutors, and whilst plea-bargaining has never existed within our laws, it has always been there, just below the surface. Defendants and defence solicitors saying they would plead guilty to something, but not to all of the matters against them. Prosecutors would then have to decide whether it was worthwhile pursuing the matters which were not to be admitted.

That analogy of a market place does not take us very far, but it is interesting to see courts as gathering points for people representing different interests in relation to the process of criminal justice.

In looking at the players within the courtroom in those days, I have already said quite a bit about magistrates in relation to their association with probation committees and the management of local probation services. But what about the magistrate of those days; who were they? In my city there was a preponderance of business owners and managers and other people of social standing, together with persons nominated by political parties and trade unions. Unlike today, where you can put yourself forward to become a magistrate, in those days you were recruited or nominated. It was in that sense, a bit like a special club. In my experience the letters J.P. (Justice of the Peace) behind one's name was a significant status symbol of those times. I like to think that my city was relatively advanced for its age, because there were many members of the bench who were not landowners or captains of industry, but were postmen and engineers from local businesses. There was a high proportion of women and, even in the 1960's, there were some people from the minority ethnic communities. However, not all benches were like that. It puts me in mind of a visit to a local rural court where the only magistrates seemed to be of the landowning class and who were still operating on out of date approaches to the dispensation of justice.

My client had a drink problem. As a result of this he was sent to a rural mental hospital for detoxification and treatment. Having progressed fairly well, he was allowed into the local community but unfortunately, got into an argument with a local person in their village library. An assault took place, and no doubt my client was responsible. I decided, however, that it was only fair of me to make an effort to attend the local court, to see if he could continue with his treatment. I attended the court and was informed about the seating arrangements for probation officers. The court clerk was clearly surprised to see a city man in their court. We were asked to rise when the bench filed in. I have already suggested that in our city court the most magistrates you are likely to see on any bench numbered three. In this case there were five; all-male, all smartly dressed, and, as I was to discover, all with views of justice slightly to the right of those of Genghis Khan. I said my piece in relation to the offender, but was completely unsurprised when the decision of the court was to remand him in custody. I would not have been surprised if they had sent me with him.

Another fascinating difference between benches was their focus on prevalent crime. In our court in the city low level matters were drunkenness and prostitution. They attracted, for the most part, modest fines. The city magistrates were aware that their "clientele" had limited incomes and fines levels were sensibly low. But, woe betides any city lads going to the surrounding country to supplement the poor rations of their family by shooting rabbits. Conviction in a rural court for "trespass in pursuit of conies", which was the charge, which allegedly upset the landowners and the local courts, were harsh. The fines were swingeing for men, with families, on benefits. I suspect that the harshness was less to do with Lord So and So being upset by losing some rabbits (who were probably a pest anyway) than it was to act as a deterrent, to any of the great unwashed from the city from even venturing into the area.

In our city, the bench of approximately 300 magistrates was divided into three rotas, one sitting every three weeks. Before each court session, morning and afternoon, Monday to Friday, an elected senior magistrate would assign those present, in the main magistrates gathering room, to different benches in order to cover each of the courts running that day. There was usually an experienced magistrate who took the chair for each bench, supported by two colleagues who were often referred to, by us, as wingers because the chair sat in the middle and the two others beside, or on the wing. One court was designated as the remand court of the day, and dealt with all the overnight matters in addition to serious matters that would ultimately end up in a higher court, like murder, rape, dwelling house burglary, et cetera. There were also the overnight summary matters such as drunk and disorderly, loitering for prostitution and the like. These cases were the ones requiring fairly straightforward decisions. In the serious cases, it was whether or not to grant bail to a defendant. In the less serious matters it was usually a matter of deciding the level of fine.

There were then one or two courts where the type of case involved more lengthy consideration. So matters that had been put off for social enquiry report, or otherwise, cases where there was likely to be lengthy mitigation from the defence, or where there was a not guilty plea and a trial was to take place, were heard in those courts. Then there was a court or two devoted entirely to motoring related matters, which formed the greatest number of all cases appearing before the courts in those days. There was also a court dedicated to the financial issues of failure to pay fines or other court financial orders. The court lists were arranged to put cases into relevant courts, and we organised our work accordingly. However, whilst each court started off with the cases allocated to it, things usually got complicated as the session progressed. Some defendants did not turn up, some solicitors were delayed, some cases took much longer than expected, some people changed their plea from guilty to not guilty at the last minute thereby obviating the need for a trial and so by about half to two thirds the way through a session, cases started to get transferred between courts.

There was always a juvenile court dealing with those under the age of 18 and above the age of 10, the latter being the age of criminal responsibility. This was located in a separate part of the building to keep the 'innocents' and their parents away from the adult criminals. Finally, there were family courts dealing with matters of the custody of children, access to children, and matters of maintenance of children. Ironically family courts used one of the courts designed for criminal cases and those attending used the same waiting area as those attending criminal courts.

Before they attended on the day, magistrates did not know the sort of matters they would be hearing, although in fairness, as time went by, the bench was subdivided into magistrates who would take a particular interest in hearing juvenile or family matters. Each magistrate was asked to attend for about 30 half day sessions a year, I believe, in other words a total of 15 whole days. So, for those employed, it did require them to have permission from their employers to undertake this task. Some magistrates did the bare minimum or thereabouts, but others with the freedom to do so, committed a great deal of time to the work of the bench, and it was this latter group which usually went on to be elected to committees of the bench. In those days the training consisted mainly of sitting with "Nelly", in other words, a more senior magistrate, and inputs from the Clerk of the Court (the principal clerk or a deputy) on law and the powers of the magistrate, and brief inputs from relevant local services like the police and the probation service.

From those who committed a lot of time to the bench, were drawn members of the various committees, such as the probation committee. On that committee in our city, when I arrived, were a number of owners of businesses and their acumen gave rise to an interesting development, which later saved a lot of money. The city hall courts that I have described were unsatisfactory and it was agreed that a new court building was to be erected. It was a potentially expensive undertaking for the Lord Chancellor's Department (LCD), who was responsible for courts. Our local probation committee did some deal with the LCD in respect of the warehouse which housed the Probation Office, and with a loan from the Home office, they part financed the building provided that the new design incorporated sufficient space to accommodate the probation staff. It was opened in the mid-1970s and initially it was very expensive for the Home office to pay the "mortgage". But that committee's decision led, some 20 or so years later to a mortgage and rent free probation office.

Another interesting point relating to my city magistrates of the day, and one which harks back to the paternalism of earlier history was the fact that they maintained a Poor Box. I referred earlier to the issue of bus fares and the Home Office provided some very meagre funds which could be used in a few cases. It will not be surprising from what I have said before that it was not my wont to use this very often. But one did come across cases where there appeared to be a genuine need which could not otherwise be met and where it was certainly not appropriate to use our Home Office funding.

Go back if you will to the case of the young woman with an outstanding 11 year old warrant. Assume, however, that instead of voluntarily coming to get the matter sorted out she had come to the attention of the police in some far distant place and even though they were not going to prosecute her they discovered the existence of the warrant. She would then have been transported at great public expense to our court. Then assuming she was dealt with in the way already described and released she might have had insufficient funds on her with which to get home many miles away.

In such scenarios the Poor Box was a great help as if the probation officer brought the plight of the woman to the attention of the court they could authorise the provision of a travel warrant to get her home. This is just one of what could be countless examples of the use of these funds. The money for the Poor Box was raised or donated by the magistrates themselves.

So far as a probation officer was concerned, contact with magistrates came about in two ways. Firstly, as I've described already, there was contact with members of the probation committee who were, technically one's employers. Additional to full committee members, if you like, the board of directors were other magistrates on the probation committee who undertook attendance at case committees. Again as previously outlined, this was a meeting where officers were required to bring individual case files, and explain to magistrates what was being done with the client and why. Magistrates had the power to require the officer to undertake particular actions where they were felt to be appropriate by the justices. As time went by, these case committees moved from the consideration of individual cases, to the consideration of general topics, which the probation service wished to bring to the attention of magistrates or about which they wished to hear. This latter development was another small nail in the coffin of the diminution of individual probation officer responsibility. When you were taking individual cases, and presenting them to case committee magistrates, there was a clear argument in favour of your status as an independent professional. As that requirement to take individual cases declined, so that link between you and your employers began to diminish.

The other way of getting to know magistrates was by appearing in court. In those days court duty was really a low level occupation; representing colleagues by either submitting their reports, getting results in cases in which they were interested, or giving general information about the work of the service, if so required, by a particular bench. But, I have indicated that for me, and many of my colleagues, appearing at court with one's reports, or in respect of one's cases, when they reoffended or breached, together with occasional court duty, led you to become known, certainly by the more senior magistrates who took the chair. Colleagues, who avoided court, were self-evidently less well known to magistrates. Right or wrong, being known, and particularly being respected, meant that your influence in relation to cases in which you were involved, or upon which you had prepared a report, was quite considerable.

Gaining the respect of the magistrates was useful, but respect was not one sided so far as I was concerned. Of course I respected them as my employers but also as unpaid representatives of their community doing a difficult job. Indeed when stipendiary magistrates became more prevalent, that is the legally trained person often a former criminal solicitor, I would always prefer a bench of magistrates because I felt the three minds were often better than one when it came to unbiased sentencing.

There were other people whom one needed to influence. I have already mentioned the court ushers. Some of my colleagues were not good at respecting the role, and potential advantage of, cultivating court ushers. This was foolish, in my view, because these folk, if onside with you, were invaluable in advising you about results in cases when you were busily engaged elsewhere, or giving you snippets of information about cases which had come up in their court, when no other member of probation staff was present. My advice to all new staff, in relation to court duty, was that they get to know the ushers, deal with them as equals, and as potentially extremely useful resources.

Then there were the court clerks. Again in those days, like probation officers, some were trained and some were not. Quite a few had gained employment in a clerical or administrative capacity in local court offices, and had gone on to some limited form of study, and with the coaching of more experienced or qualified staff, had become fully fledged court clerks. The role was an interesting one. They were there to advise the magistrates on the law as it pertained to each case. There was great reliance upon Stones Justices Manual, a huge tome which was regularly updated as new legal provisions were enacted. Quite properly, in due course, the role became designated as legal advisers, with the requirement that they did have legal training. Incidentally, in the Crown Court, the court clerk even to this day is not required to be legally trained, and they are properly called court clerks, and not legal advisers. A legally trained person is not needed as a clerk in Crown Court because the Judge is so trained.

Regular attendance by the probation officer at court, and cultivating court clerks during periods of magisterial recess, was important. If you had a report case, or a breach case, and you wanted to get it heard as early in the particular session as was possible, to enable you to get away and do other work, your relationship with the court clerk was crucial. Of course, local solicitors usually took precedence, but aside from that, if you were known and respected by the court clerk, they would usually call your case on earlier than occasional visitors to the court, including solicitors from out of town.

Also, if you were respected by the court clerk and the magistrates, I suspect that on occasion an allusion to the regard in which the probation officer was held became a significant factor when the justices were considering particularly difficult case decisions. The magistrates retired alone to a private room to consider their decision. However, they frequently called upon the court clerk whose role, in theory, was simply to make reference to the legal parameters at issue, but in my opinion they undoubtedly influenced decisions from time to time, where the bench was split or unsure.

Prosecutors, were normally members of the police force in those days but, as we moved into the 1970s and beyond, cities like ours, employed prosecuting solicitors, I think we had two. By and large they dealt with the more complex matters, but also staffed the remand court, where amongst the serious cases, destined for the higher courts, there was the low level overnight case. I do remember one in particular prosecutor, whose presentation of cases of drunkenness needed to be seen to be believed.

Imagine, if you will, one of those end of pier machines, into which you can insert a coin and then by use of small leavers manipulate a mechanical arm to try to capture a stuffed toy. At the dropping of the coin the arm comes to life you move it to try and grab a stuffed animal, but whether you succeed or not, the arm then rises of its own volition to its full height and swings over the shoot from which the animal would drop, if you were lucky enough to catch one. It would then immediately sink back to its resting position. So it was with this prosecutor in cases of simple drunkenness, as he started to speak he rose slowly, unfurling his back and legs, eventually becoming ramrod straight. As soon as his back and legs were straight, and he was fully upright, he immediately began the slow reverse decent to take his seat. The words spoken during this seamless rise and fall, went something like this "Eleven fifteen yesterday evening, the 20th March, your worships, the defendant was in Town Street. He was unsteady on his feet, his eyes were glazed, and he smelt strongly of intoxicants. He was drunk your worships". The whole delivery took less than 30 seconds and was usually followed by the regulation fine of the day and the whole case was concluded within a couple of minutes.

Defence solicitors, on the other hand were people with whom we, in those days, had much more contact. They were as varied in their individual professional approach, as we probation officers. No doubt they found some of us more approachable than others; those feelings were reciprocated. There was to a certain extent, a tension between their role and ours. They may have briefly seen their client in the cells, or indeed, they may have passed that duty over to a junior clerk, who had simply briefed them. But very often they had limited information, other than in relation to the present offence, about the background of the people that they represented, particularly in cases arrested, and held overnight. There were some solicitors who regularly represented the same defendant on his repeat offending, and in those cases they obviously knew a lot more. However, with our own cases the tension was that they were very keen to hear how their client was doing on probation, and if you were not careful you provided them with their whole mitigation, and it seemed as though they were far more knowledgeable about the client than was actually the case. They might also omit the less flattering parts of our information concerning their client. As time went by my technique was to say yes, he is on probation and not doing too badly, but before you mitigate about the offence, put me into bat, in the witness box, and I'll tell the court how is doing. This then gained credit for the service rather than the solicitor.

I cannot leave mention of solicitors without reference to Desmond. He was, in my view, one of the characters of the court in my early days. His firm of solicitors took a lion's share of the criminal work coming before our courts. He was a flamboyant character. Saturday morning courts were held for cases where the person had been remanded from the night before, and if the court had not run on a Saturday they would have remained in police custody until the Monday. Where a person was held in custody, the police or the offender would contact their solicitor and they would turn up on the Saturday morning to plead for bail, or whatever. The standard of male dress before the courts in those days was quite clear, suit, shirt, and tie, and normally of fairly conservative colours. Regularly on a Saturday, Desmond would appear in brightly a coloured check shirt, open necked, with vividly coloured corduroy trousers. His first comment to the bench was always "Your Worships, I profoundly apologise for my appearance. I had just got to the golf course when I received the request to attend here". Complete lie of course, but that was his style.

Two regular elements of Desmond's mitigation are worth commenting upon. He always referred to the disadvantage of a client. It is no longer politically correct but, he would use phrases like "he is of gypsy stock" or "sadly he comes from a rural Irish background" - even though Desmond was Irish himself - as though this in some way excused any behaviour that his client might have undertaken. And then there were those nonsensical comments allegedly ascribed to sages of the past. Representing a young man, whom he was trying to establish as the lesser participant of the two young men in the dock, he came out with the following. "Your Worships, as Confucius says, when one nail stands higher than the other, the wrath of the hammer shall fall heaviest on the higher nail". I have made no particular study of Confucius and his sayings, but, I am very doubtful whether that was one that Confucius ever postulated.

In Shakespeare's Henry IV, Part 1, Act III Scene 2 whilst passing through Rouen market place Joan la Pucelle (aka Joan of Arc) says *"Take heed, be wary how you place your words;"* and that is probably good advice in any Court setting too.

So in this marketplace, the "traders" who came together represented different points of view which immediately created a tension between one another. You therefore had to ensure that you were clear about your own role and responsibilities, and you had to stand up for yourself and your service against the views of these other people. Almost conversely, you also had to learn to work together, to create alliances, and to show respect to the others involved. As my initial story in this chapter shows, whilst many of us were there to argue a cause, which might be contrary to the views of others, there was nevertheless a reasonable camaraderie amongst those of us coming together regularly when the court doors opened. In my view the court work role was a fascinating one and it is perhaps no coincidence, that I spent the latter half of my working life having responsibility for, and operating in, the provision of probation services in court settings.

Chapter 16
Home Visits

"An Englishman's home is his castle". Proverb

*

Joe was in his late twenties but still lived at home with his dad. Part of his offending related to his unhappy relationship with his father, but he was unwilling to move out of the family home because he was unemployed and really couldn't afford it. So, it seemed to me, when we were creating the work plan, that home visits, and the involvement of dad, was important and this was agreed with both of them, on the basis that one office visit by Joe this week, would be followed by my visiting their home, to see them both, the next.

There was a problem, and in fairness they did warn me about it; it was Blackie the dog.

Dad's house was on a city council estate where crime may not have been rife but was certainly an issue that householders needed to take into account. Joe's dad, perhaps more concerned with suffering burglary than most, had located a rather large cupboard behind the front door, meaning that the only easy access to the home, without breaking a window, was via the back door. To further deter any potential burglars, Blackie the dog was deployed as a sentry. Now Blackie was of mixed parentage. There was definitely a bit of Alsatian in there, but also another large dog. He was not far off the size of your average small bear, or so it seemed to me.

Blackie was secured in the garden by means of a sturdy chain, attached at one end to his collar, and at the other nailed into a fence post. The length of the chain was such that Blackie could only reach a point about two or three feet from the back door, although an unwitting intruder would not know that. Joe was careful to explain to me that I could not enter through the front door when I came, and that I had to proceed down the side of the building to the back door.

He told me that Blackie's infallible hearing would detect my approach, and that I would hear a fearsome barking, and when I turned the corner to get to the back door Blackie would undoubtedly leave his kennel by the back fence and charge across the garden towards me. The technique for entry, I was told, was to keep close against the wall and then push open the back door and enter.

With some trepidation I made my first approach. Down the side of the building and already there was loud barking, I reached the corner whereupon Blackie charged across the garden towards me being pulled up short, as promised, by the chain. Creeping by the wall, I got to the back door and entered successfully. That first visit was followed by several more, and on each occasion, I followed the prescribed method of approach. I suppose that after a few visits, I became somewhat blasé.

One day, I approached the house in order to make my visit. Down the side of the house; commencement of barking; turn the corner; Blackie charges; the chain pulls him up short, and as usual raises him off the ground by his neck, whereupon the nail holding the chain to the fence, having suffered many brutal tugs in the past, finally gives up the ghost and comes out.

Fortunately for me, my reaction in taking the two further steps to the back door was marginally faster than the astounded Blackie's realisation that, he could, and should, have got me.

*

Leaving aside childhood birthday parties, visits to play with neighbours' children, and trips to see elderly relatives, many adults will have limited experience of entering other people's homes. A lot of physical social contact (as opposed to the online type) takes place in pubs, and clubs, and restaurants. It is, therefore, for most people, an unusual experience to visit a new home. Such visits to different houses happened to me on average about every week or two of my working life. The opposite side of that coin is that many people like to control whom they invite into their house, perhaps following the old adage, quoted above, that 'an Englishman's home is his castle'.

I have already indicated that visiting homes was mainly directed at seeing those 'significant others' in an offender's life. It did, however, also yield other information regarding the lifestyle in that household. How did people interact with one another, how many people were there, did it seem likely that other agencies were involved with the family, and a whole range of other questions were either posed, or answered, by being within that household. But at the same time one had to respect the fact that you were a visitor, albeit an official one, and that you should try to be as unobtrusive as possible. Yet at the same time you had a job to do, and on occasions things like asking for the TV the to be turned off were reasonable, if controlling, mechanisms in making it clear that this was an important matter, and should be treated as such by all concerned.

Looking back, visits were predominantly, but by no means entirely, to local authority council housing or rented accommodation. There was then a reasonable proportion of owner occupied houses, but I cannot recall visiting many large detached properties. By the 1960s council estates in our city were well developed and quite large. In my patch, the north-east segment of the city, there were six council estates, one of which was by far the biggest. The accommodation in these estates consisted mainly of semi-detached houses with, additionally, a significant number of low rise maisonettes. On the biggest estate there was one massive medium rise block of about 12 stories. In regard to this latter block, there was, in those days, no restriction upon those entering and consequently, even though lifts were provided, they were frequently out of order due to vandalism. You then had to trudge up several flights of stairs to reach the floor you required, on the way dodging stray dogs (or evidence that they had been there) and stray teenagers.

Each estate had its own identity, differing from neighbouring estates, which may be situated only the other side of a main arterial route. Also, the sub cultures which developed on each of the estates differed from others. The subculture of an estate could also change with time, as one generation of, let us say criminals, gave way to the next. It was important to be aware of the nuances of each estate and take that into account with the person with whom you were dealing.

I would hate it if any of the above implied that I had some 'holier than thou' attitude to people living on council estates. Some of the cheeriest and warmest feeling homes I have ever been privileged to enter have been households on estates. But, I am afraid that the reputation of estates went before the offenders who appeared in court. It was therefore important for probation officers to put into context the social milieu in which the offender lived, and in particular to point out the positives of families, youth and other local organisations, that were contributing helpfully to the life of their own community.

Another part of the housing stock much visited, were the back-to-back and terraced houses of the inner city. The rear house was accessed through an alleyway. The front door usually opened on to the main living area which was not very large, often with stone steps leading to a cellar and sometimes this incorporated the kitchen. Also, rising out of the front room were the steps to the upstairs two bedrooms, one of which would be partially built over the alleyway. The conditions in these homes were pretty primitive, but by and large people living in them experienced a positive community life. In my personal view, they provided a better quality of life than those being rehoused into the high-rise blocks which were then so popular. I cannot remember who did the research, but I do remember reading about the fact that most human beings, in looking for an ideal home, want a 'defensible space', which included some outside space, and albeit these back to backs were very small, there was a small garden at the back together, in some cases, with the toilet facilities.

Finally, again within the older stock of housing, we had a number of large inner-city Victorian houses which had once been the province of owners, or managers, of big businesses. As their former owners had moved outwards, so entrepreneurs had arrived, bought up the properties, subdivided them into small bedsits, and proceeded to charge the earth for renting them out. I remember one particular area where all the houses had been converted in this way by one landlord. He then employed a man called Jack who was responsible for managing the properties. Effectively he would take anybody who brought the money for the rent and paid it one week in advance. At the end of the week they would need to pay for the next week or Jack would be round to collect next week's money, and if you did not have it then you were required to leave. Whether or not it was strictly legal was perhaps not something to which the person staying in the accommodation gave consideration when faced by Jack and his very ferocious two Alsatian dogs.

Rent control has had a mixed history in this country and certainly between the mid-50s in the mid-60s it was not in operation, as I understand, but after it was re-imposed it was very helpful to the sort of clients who lived in bedsit land, that we had on our books. I know that subsequently rent control has disappeared from the statute books, but as I write this in the middle of the second decade of the 21st-century, it seems to me that some form of management of the rented housing market may be helpful.

So, I would say, that visiting most homes, one found generally good conditions of living. Material provision may not always have been that good, but there were fairly few homes that were dirty and unhygienic. In the early 1970s I was asked to have a prison officer, from a local open prison, on attachment for a week, to observe the work that we did. Of course I took him to court, and he sat in with me during reporting sessions, but, it was also important for him to see the work that I did by visiting homes. Most of these were homes that were in good condition, but, I was at the time working with one family living in a very damp inner-city house that was due for demolition in the not too distant future. Father was unemployed, as I recall it, with a bad back, mother was careworn and whilst I was dealing with their son, a young man in middle teens, there were much younger siblings one of whom was certainly under three.

In those days it was my practice, which remained fairly well unchanged for most of my career, to wear suits of brown or green, because I felt that that made me stand out when I went to court as not being among the solicitor types, who always wore dark or pinstripe suits in those days. Also these colours seemed to me to be less threatening when visiting homes. I liked to see these suits as my 'chameleon garb'; blending me into a variety of situations in which I might find myself, on any given day. My prison officer came every day in immaculately pressed grey trousers, I think he had been in the military before the prison service, and a smart brass buttoned blazer with crisp white shirt and tie. Sartorially he obviously put me to shame. However, when we came to the damp house mentioned above, I was invited in and introduced the prison officer, (I had previously warned the family that my next visit would include somebody in training), and I promptly went to sit on the settee. Although invited to sit the prison officer student stood behind the settee, almost I felt, at attention, during this particular interview.

When we left I asked what he thought about the visit and he remarked that he was amazed that I could go in and sit down in such a house, particularly as he thought that the little child, who was running round without any lower clothes on, may have wet the settee. I tried to explain to him, I think in vain, that if I'd gone in and stood up throughout I would not, in my social work sense, have really been engaging with those people, I would have been talking at them, rather than to and with them. I accepted that on occasion it was important to take note and be sure to sit on the dry end of the settee. But for me standing would not have been an option.

One particular personal difficulty I had during my time of making home visits, was that I have an allergy to cats. This is not an insignificant matter. If a cat touches me with its claws I will get red wheals on my skin, if I touch a cat and then touch some piece of skin, such as on my face or neck it will become very irritable and on one occasion, although nothing to do with clients, I stayed in the home of a relative who had cats, and became very asthmatic after only a relatively short period. Amazingly, if I went to a home with a cat then that feline would almost inevitably make a beeline for me. Now, if not sitting down in somebody's house might cause mild offence, then shooing away their favourite moggy was even worse. I found the only way that I could deal with it, whenever I noticed that a cat was part of the household, was to tell the truth about my allergy at the very beginning and then it did not usually cause a problem.

Considerations of health and safety in terms of home visiting were really not on the horizon in those days. That is not to say we were stupid or blasé about visiting people who were known to be violent or unpredictable. But, I cannot think of any case of those days that would have worried me in terms of making a visit to their home on my own. Yes, there were occasions where you had to be authoritarian, particularly in respect of breach of orders, but, by and large, you held a role that was seen by clients as being non-threatening, and broadly based in a desire to help them. Because of this, they were rarely in a position to feel angry with you; that is not to say you did not find them angry on occasions but that was often with the court, another agency, or just life.

Although issues of security, and health and safety, developed in the 1980s, our city office did not have to have a security grille, for the receptionist, until about the time that the original probation order went out of existence. I suppose what I'm saying is that after the end of the probation order, or at the very least in the period leading up to that demise, the ethos of the probation service was changed subtly, to become less cooperative with the offender and more confrontational to him. This was a centrally decided, top down, managerially driven decision which together with the removal of consent to the making of a probation order proved a final assault on the role of independent professional probation officer working in a tripartite contract with court and client.

Chapter 17
Offenders and Mental Illness

"A sick thought can devour the body's flesh more than fever or consumption."
Guy de Maupassant

*

He should never have been made subject to a probation order, but there was no mental health facility that was able to take him at the time of the making of the order. Stephen was in his late teens, and had come before the courts for a very minor matter of damage. The court was, rightly, concerned about him, since it was evident from his demeanour in court that he was, in the parlance of the day, simpleminded.

I forget now why he was on his own, whether or not the family had kicked him out or could no longer cope with him. Either way he was a very vulnerable young man. I wrote the social enquiry report and recommended that he be seen by a psychiatrist, all the while, he was temporarily housed in a local hostel. The psychiatric report confirmed the need for treatment or rather, residence, in a facility that was designed to meet his needs. Sadly there was no such facility with a current vacancy. Despite the court making one further adjournment, to see if a place would become available, it did not and they could not go on indefinitely adjourning and not concluding the matter. It was therefore decided that a probation order would be made, to support him in the interim, pending the availability of an appropriate place.

By negotiation with the Social Security office, and given that the hostel could no longer keep him, we found him a place in one of the bedsits in an old Victorian house which had been converted to that purpose. Social Security agreed to pay his rent, we arranged for him to have a daily meal at a voluntary organisation and I, together with a probation volunteer, tried our best to support him. Contact was arranged on the basis that I would see him twice a week in my office and once at his home, the volunteer visited on at least two of the days when I did not see him. You can see that his level of need was pretty high.

Now, I should perhaps explain that despite all the difficulties we were experiencing in trying to organise something satisfactory for Stephen, he was absolutely delighted with what we were doing for him. This delight was manifest by the sheer pleasure which appeared on his face whenever we met, usually accompanied by his jumping up and down or shaking with excitement. He displayed these traits of excitement when I saw him in the office. He did the same when I saw him at his home. Sometimes even, this was followed by a hug from him, which was difficult to resist or escape.

The bedsit was of pretty poor quality, and I was not very pleased with it, but it was supposed to be a short-term solution and there was no obvious alternative. On about my second or third visit, I arrived outside the old Victorian house, parked the car, and started towards the series of steep stone steps which led to the front door. Before ascending the steps I looked up to see Stephen coming out of the front door carrying a bowl brimming with a viscous looking liquid. I was at the bottom of the steps; Stephen the top. He glanced down and saw me. Immediate his excitable shaking cheerfulness took over and the bowl visibly wobbled in his hand.

"Hello", he said, "Toilets broken".

"Please put the bowl down, Stephen." I said retreating smartly.

*

From a lay perspective mental illness or disorder generally causes the sufferer to experience a significantly different reality from others and from society's norm. Sufferers often behave, and in some cases, look different, and their presentation, or behaviour, or actions, set them apart from their fellows. One part of that 'difference' may be that they fail to observe societal rules and sometimes that leads to transgressions of the law. Occasionally these transgressions can be dealt with informally, because those enforcing the law recognise that the actions were born of a distorted perception. Much later on, post 1985, when the Crown Prosecution Service was created, it devised two tests for embarking on a prosecution. The Evidential Test was about ensuring that there was sufficient evidence to justify a prosecution. The second test was the Public Interest Test. This test could then be used where a mental illness was clearly evident, to stop the prosecution unless it was felt to be in the public interest, that is to say, the offence was of sufficient seriousness to warrant going before the courts, or there was persistence in offending.

I do remember a young man, again one of limited capacity, who, with the appropriate support, managed his life fairly well and had settled accommodation in a local authority hostel. His primary problem was that he had an extremely low threshold of coping with frustration. When life was going well for him, as it did most of the time, there was not a problem. But whenever he experienced a frustration, of whatever sort, he seemed only to be able to alleviate that new frustration by breaking windows. Not just any old window. It had to be something significant like a shop or door window. His preferred method of breaking windows, in his frustrated state, was to stand in front of them with his back to the glass and kick back until they broke. Perhaps nowadays glass is stronger, but in those days he could quite easily make a mess of a shop front. He came on probation, although not to me, and advances were made, but at the end of the day this behaviour seemed to be incurable. The frequency of offending, the significant values of replacing the glass meant that, after the first few times of letting him off because of his mental condition, the courts could no longer go on trying to reform him. Eventually, despite his vulnerability imprisonment was used.

This client, and the client Stephen at the beginning of this section, were individuals with lack of capacity. Incidentally, the terminology of those days is quite interesting, we did not use the concept of mental capacity then, but there were two labels, namely, sub-normality and severe sub-normality, the second of which, from memory, involved a person assessed with an IQ of less than 70. But aside from issues of mental capacity, there was proper mental illness. Either way, people with issues of capacity, or mental illness, or disorder were common amongst our caseload of the day.

Prior to the 1960s there was a move to treat people with significant issues of capacity or mental ill-health in large psychiatric hospitals. One of those serving our city was immense. It has in recent years been redeveloped into a full-scale village of its own, incorporating the original huge buildings adapted into luxury flats, and the building of many new homes in the huge area of land that was around it. Just along the road is a graveyard with a plaque that reads *"This site is the last resting place of 2,858 patients of ....Hospital who died between1905-1969. May they rest in peace"*. Beginning in the 1960s there was a move to de-institutionalisation, and no longer was it easy for courts to deal with a person with mental illnesses or capacity by sending the offender back to the hospital. Suddenly, the courts had to deal with these cases by other means, and of course they, understandably, looked to the probation service for help.

It is difficult to quantify, especially in retrospect, but I have no doubt that my caseload would normally contain between 10 and 20% of people with capacity or mental illness issues. For some of them we could work with local psychiatrists, but they, like us, were under an increasing workload pressure. Many of the people with the difficulties I am referring to were a problem for the police as well. They may have accommodation problems and a further offence might make a family decide that they could no longer cope with that individual. Whilst the police have long held a duty of care and responsibility for taking people with mental problems that are significant, or florid, to a "place of safety", they too were struggling to deal with the numbers of such people committing offences, and for them, in many cases, the best way was to hand the problem over to the courts.

So many clients with these sorts of problems do I recall. Some of those not mentioned elsewhere in this diatribe include Norman, a middle-class man, so paranoid that even in the 1970s he had to record all our meetings on a Dictaphone so that he could, if necessary at a later date, in his terms defend himself. David, apprehended alone muttering in a back garden outside a wooden shed, after the householder had called the police and they approached him, they recorded him saying as his first response to their request to know what he was doing, "me and my mate are shifting this wardrobe"; I'm sure he would have believed that statement in his view of reality, even though to the relatively sane police officer that was patently untrue. John who was on probation to a colleague for buggery of a horse; suffering from very limited mental capacity and sadly, in retrospect, the butt of office jokes that went along the lines of 'was the horse tethered' and did it say "nay"'.

On the other hand mental illness in particular could be susceptible to treatment. One client upon whom I wrote a report had been convicted of a serious offence of arson in which he had effectively burned down his childhood school. When I first met Richard he was clearly mentally unwell and as 'Arson with Intent to Endanger Life' carried a life imprisonment maximum sentence, his position was serious. The psychiatric report recommended a secure mental hospital and that is where he went for several years. He was successfully treated and after a long period of monitoring was released subject to a Conditional Discharge from the Hospital, to which he could be instantly returned at the first sign of relapse. I supervised him for about 6 years after his release at the end of which I reported that he no longer needed supervision, as he had demonstrated that he was unlikely to relapse and that he was leading a settled life. I was also confident that his supportive family would inform the authorities if there were problems. Ten years later I met him by chance at a petrol station and he was still doing well.

In respect of the cases of mental illness, and lack of capacity, in those days, probation officers were called upon to bail out courts, who faced difficult decisions. We worked with a fairly small and under pressure psychiatric service. Essentially however we were applying a sticking plaster to the political decisions that had led to the abolition of the large mental hospitals, without fully resourcing community services to effectively deal with many of these people.

Chapter 18
Opinion

"Your work is to discover your work and then with all your heart to give yourself to it."   Buddha

*

Have I succeeded then? Have I painted a picture of the probation officer in, what I have described as, the heydays of that role? There will be some readers, who are of my vintage, and who may take exception to my description of the role. To them, and any other sceptic, I can only say this, that this is how I firstly approached and viewed my work and also I felt that this view and understanding of role was broadly shared and reflected in the work of my predecessors who taught me and colleagues of the day, in our city.

In our Social Enquiry Reports of those heydays, we always ended with a paragraph entitled "Conclusion". At the time, it seemed appropriate to use that term; it was the concluding part of the report in which you drew together, what, in your independent opinion, were the major points and went on to suggest your view of "the most suitable sentence" for the client. I have to confess that much later, and probably long after those heydays but before reports became formulaic, I concluded my reports to court with a paragraph entitled "Opinion". I did so because that seemed to me to better reflect the fact that, independent professional or not, what I was doing was to postulate my view, and although my opinion was, given all the efforts I had made to enquire, inquire and verify, still just one view. The final view was to be taken by others with wider responsibilities and the legal decision making duty.

And so it is here. I have set out the basis of my 'report' and now I will move to conclude, or rather to offer an opinion.

The role of the probation officer, from its inception in 1907, was, in broad terms, to act as an unbiased reporter to, and social worker for, the courts. The courts themselves covered many relatively small geographical areas up until the changes brought about in part by the local government reorganisation of 1974. Those local courts were originally given the responsibility of the oversight of the work of their local probation service, which, certainly from 1948 onwards, was overseen in the broadest terms by a principal probation officer whom I have called a first among equals rather than a manager of the work of staff, in the terms which were to evolve in later years. Local magistrates' courts, or at least some of the magistrates elected by their peers to the purpose, took a particular interest in the work of the probation service including to the point of hiring and firing probation officers. There was a frequent and relatively detailed contact between magistrates and probation officers, and magistrates retained the power to make specific recommendations as to how a probation officer might deal with a case, until the 1970s.

The probation order itself developed from 1907, but the 1948 Criminal Justice Act was a watershed and created the climate that existed in what I have claimed to be the heydays for the role of the independent professional probation officer, in the 1950s, 1960s and 1970s. I have argued that in those days the probation order was a tripartite contract between court, offender and probation officer, with the latter having the role of monitoring the adherence of the probationer to the order and reporting any infractions of the order to the court. Furthermore, because of this 'contract management' role, together with being employees of the local magistrates, and given that the probation hierarchy of the day was instructed to be supportive rather than managerial, I have argued that the role of probation officer in those times was clearly that of an independent, professional.

That was the service, and role, into which I stepped in the 1960s. I had responsibility learned from my professional training to deal with my clients by reference to a very clear set of social work principles. Clients were to be respected, irrespective of the nature of their offending. Clients deserved confidentiality, to be listened to, to be faced with consequences of their offending and to be helped to devise ways of avoiding further offending and to improve their lives, so far as was possible.

Despite working within the social work principles, I was nevertheless committed to respecting the wishes and requirements of the court and the specific orders which it made. Sometimes, there was a conflict between clients' need and court requirement; in such circumstances the latter, so far as I was concerned, took precedence and I am sure that was so for many of my colleagues of the day.

Lives and societies are not static, they move on, they develop and it becomes a matter of opinion as to whether or not those developments are good or bad. What I do know is that a cult of managerialism took hold in the probation service in the 1980s and at the same time there was a wider political belief in centralisation of management of public bodies. These two factors came together to put pressure on considering reducing the involvement of local courts in the management of the probation service and handing it over to managers who would better reflect the views of centre.

These developments in the 1980's and 90's began to turn what I have argued was the independent probation officer role established in 1948 into one of an increasingly fully managed, centre driven prescribed role which consequently led to a diminishing ability to act independently.

But just as with the inception of the probation order in 1907, these internal changes came at the time of a radical review of sentencing principles and arrangements. This review led to the 1991 Criminal Justice Act, which I have pointed out, brought to the end the option of a Probation Order as a sentence to be used by the courts. I was as vociferous as the next person, in those days, about the proposed loss of the name of probation officer as a result of that act, those objections were upheld and the name retained. Really I now acknowledge that I was wrong and we should have moved to a different name at that point, because why should you have a probation officer, if there is no such thing as a probation order?

I remained in the probation service for a total of 34 years and continued to work as a self-employed court skills and advocacy trainer with many members of probation staff for a further twelve. I enjoyed all of the years pre-1991 and post, but I do look back on the 1960s and 1970s as being the heyday years of the independent professional probation officer role. It is because of that view, that I have felt it important to reflect, what I believe, may be the views and attitudes of myself, my immediate predecessors who taught me and many close colleagues, of that time.

Just like the efforts of King Canute it was impossible to stem the tidal assault on the independence of the probation officer role by the increasingly politically centre driven managerialism. After years of training new staff and managing services to local courts, but doing regular duties myself to keep my hand in and to ensure staff knew what I was talking about, I decided to leave the low level management role of senior probation officer and return to the "shop floor". I spent my final years of service as a probation officer in my local courts, advising magistrates and judges about the circumstances of offenders and giving opinions as to possible options for dealing with them. New requirements from centre constrained the role but it was as near as I could get to the independence I had originally enjoyed.

In my contention I stepped into an independent professional probation officer role when I was given that first job by the nice lady with the hat; and looking back they were the heydays for that role. I always held my local magistrates in high regard, even though I sometimes disagreed with their decisions and I always saw my relationship with them as important because, I suppose, it had been in those heydays when I set out. Then local magistrates would have seen me as 'their' officer. So whilst colleagues were kind and generous to me on my retirement the undoubtedly greatest treasured gift was the plaque, presented to me by the then Chair of the Bench with the inscription *"With grateful thanks for over 30 years' service to the city courts"*.

Finally, at the start of this chapter and in relation to the quotation from Bhudda, I went through a few other occupations before I found in his terms 'my work'. I then did "give my heart" to it. In doing so I was richly rewarded with the opportunity to work with many committed colleagues, sentencers, court users and most of all I was privileged to be involved with so many clients and hopefully to have helped a good few of those to improve their lives.

Appendices

Appendix 1

Case example - Billy Hall

I have chosen to provide one expansive case example. It concerns well over eleven years of involvement, from 1970 to the early 1980s, with Billy Hall (not his real name). I have chosen this case for several reasons. It covers a part of the heyday period I am writing about. It involves a man with mental capacity problems, who also had an addiction – in his case to alcohol. And because of this drunkenness issue, it harks back to the role of those original probation officers. I hope that you will enjoy reading about Billy as much as I enjoyed being part of his life.

Sadly we must start with his funeral.

It was a beautiful, sunny, spring morning as Eric, our office receptionist, and I drove out of the city towards the church where the funeral was to take place. We arrived at the car park near the church and looked at the beautiful display of pretty yellow daffodils, in the council maintained flowerbeds beside the car park. "Sad it should come to this", I said to Eric. "Yes", he agreed, "We will miss him." Billy had been my client for over 11 years, a very frequent visitor to the office, and when I was out, which was quite often because he rarely came at appointment times but whenever his spirit moved him. Eric, between his other duties, spent a lot of time talking to him. "Remind me, said Eric where did it all begin?"

Eleven years previously, in 1969 I had been allocated a social enquiry report on a man then aged about 37, who had been remanded in custody to the local prison for three weeks, and I was to prepare the report. Our local prison, a Victorian built one, had one of those sets of wonderful 20 foot high wooden gates, which opened only to admit prison vehicles, and into the bottom of one of the doors was cut a six-foot high door for the admission of visitors coming on foot.

119

In those days one made a booking to visit a prisoner and, after being identified and booked in at the gate, you were taken to a special visits room, normally reserved for the visits of people like solicitors and probation officers. I entered the room and selected a desk and awaited, with interest, my first sight of Billy.

He entered the room, asked the officer in charge whom he was supposed to be seeing, and was pointed in my direction. He was about five foot six in height, lean, with wiry and fading ginger hair. He walked towards me in something of a mincing gait and greeted me with a fairly traditional prisoners greeting of the day. "Have you got a fag?" I was a non-smoker, so I said that I couldn't assist him which resulted in the pouting of his lips, and a look which said 'then you're of no use to me mate'. I explained that the court had remanded him in custody on this offence of burglary of commercial premises, and that before he was sentenced they wanted to know more about him. The papers indicated that although this was a low value matter, Billy was homeless and the court was concerned about him, no doubt partly because it was then winter. I explained that before we could discuss what might happen at court, I would need to understand something of his background, and so with his acquiescence, I took out my pen and began to make notes of his social history.

He had been born the youngest of eight children. From what I could gather, family circumstances had not been good. His father was a general dealer, essentially a "rag and bone" man who plied his trade with a horse and cart, and the family income was both low and variable. Mother appears to have been a careworn lady who died when Billy was only in his mid-teens. One thing I noted at the time, which was to become somewhat ironically significant, was that a sister, who had taken a large share of the care Billy in his younger years, and to whom I sensed he was close, had subsequently died in a house fire. After mother's death Billy stayed at home with dad, as gradually all his other siblings left. Most of them lived in the city but there was very limited contact between Billy and them. It would appear that he had blotted his copy book with each of them and they were no longer willing to support him.

About six months before the commission of this offence Billy's father had died, in his 80s. It became clear that Billy had been unable to manage his life subsequently. The house in which father had been renting passed, in terms of tenancy, to Billy, but he been unable to maintain the payments and had also allowed it to become a real mess and ultimately he was given his marching orders. There followed a few months of dossing with friends and relatives until he 'muckied his ticket' with everyone he knew and was reduced to sleeping rough.

His previous offending record was very limited. There had been an offence of theft many years previously, but other than that there were only two recent offences of drunkenness on his record. The circumstances of the present offence were these; he had slept in the doorway of a corner shop in a very poor area of the city. The prosecution case was that he had entered it by breaking into the front door, although it later transpired that somebody else had broken in and Billy, in a state of intoxication, had found the door open and entered. Billy's version was that he lent against the door and it flew open, and whilst he did enter the building he didn't do anything wrong.

My assessment was a man of limited intelligence, although very streetwise, and a lack of capacity to be able to manage very well without the guidance of some authority figure, as his father had been. He needed clear rules of guidance and practical assistance of managing his day-to-day living arrangements. I believed that a short period on probation would be useful to ensure that he got into accommodation and was helped to set up and regularise managing his income and daily life.

It seems amazing, looking back, that within the 10 days or so that would elapse after the interview, the city housing department would be able to offer him a one bedroomed flat, not long after the date of the court appearance. He had previously not held a council tenancy, so there was nothing against him so far as they were concerned, and when I explained the courts concern about him to them they were most helpful. So it was arranged that immediately after the court hearing he would spend a few nights in the local Salvation Army hostel pending the flat being furnished. There was to be a small grant from Social Security, and the local Catholic Housing Aid Society provided some basic furnishings and a Baby Belling cooker.

Before court I went to the police station cells to see Billy to tell him all that I had arranged and he was delighted and he agreed that he would be willing to be placed on probation. When we got to Court I presented my report, indicating the work that I had done and the plan for his accommodation. I proposed a probation order and the court asked Billy if he would agree to being placed on probation, and he said he would. The actual order said that he was placed on Probation for two years for the offence of "entering a commercial premises and stealing therein 5 lollipops and 3 toffees". You may find this hard to believe but I kept a copy of this order for many years (with the name and personal details redacted). I gather that the police were concerned about him but an offence of just trespass would not have resulted in the matter of his accommodation being sorted out. So the shopkeeper said that he thought a few sweets might have been taken and thus the charge was made.

And so there commenced a period of supervision which was to last for the next 11 years, until his death. Only the first part and two brief later parts involved him being on probation, for the most part he availed himself of the facility of 'voluntary after-care' in respect of his releases, on various occasions, from short prison sentences.

That first probation order was a rollercoaster. The initial arrangements, to which I referred, were excellent. I spent a lot of time, with the help of a probation volunteer, dealing with the practical side of things. His flat, aside from the bare floorboards, was adequately furnished, he had a good roof over his head, means of cooking and, whilst it was by no means physically perfect, it was quite adequate, especially if you compare it to rough sleeping. If there was a problem with the council flat, it was that, as I later realised, this particular block was something of a dumping ground for the 'difficult cases'. Billy lived next door to Francis. Francis was a domineering alcoholic considerably older than Billy, and he soon became a substitute, unhelpful, father figure, and a greater significance in Billy's life than myself and the volunteer.

Managing money was always going to be an issue and soon it became clear that, as his rent began to go into arrears, due to the negative influence of Francis, that his accommodation was at risk and that without accommodation he would be back to sleeping rough and liable to commit crime to survive. As I have said, he was a man whose capacity was less than others, and he had, for far too long in his life, submitted to the guidance, if not direction, of his father. So when the eviction notice arrived, and in a sober moment and facing the reality of life on the streets again, I got his agreement to his money being paid via the office and that I would help him manage it. On the social work principle that the client should be responsible for self-determination and workers should only advise, not take the decisions, it was unusual for us, or indeed me, to arrange for Social Security to be paid in this way but this case seemed to be an exception. So his cheque arrived weekly and he would go to the post office, cash it and pay rent and other dues. He then brought the balance to me for safekeeping till the middle of the week when he would come for his 'second instalment'.

It had worked well for a few months. Increasingly, however, it was obvious that he was drinking more and more. The normal tipple of the alcoholic of those days was cheap cider, which could be purchased in big bottles at a very low price. More and more frequently, he was coming back a day, or two days, before the due date of the second part of his money. Matters came to a head one day when he came and asked for his money and it was only the day after he had received his first half of the week's amount. I refused and he became aggressive and went away. Shortly afterwards there was a knock at my door, Billy stood there with a policeman who said that Billy had stated that I had stolen his money. We discussed the matter and I accepted that the money which I held was not mine, it was his and I felt that it was important now that he had gone this far, that I returned him this money, but that I did so with a warning, in front of the officer, that I could no longer continue our money arrangement, and that this might cause problems for him, but so be it.

Unsurprisingly it didn't take very long before, now managing his own finances, he was again facing eviction, he was knocking at my door drunk demanding money from me which of course I could no longer give him, because of the changed arrangement. Visits to the office varied in their nature. There was the crying drunk mode where he would babble on about his father and he would cry before pleading for money (It put me in mind of George the NADPAS man mentioned earlier, who's standard comment to crying drunks was "Go on son, cry all you want, the more you cry the less you pee"). Then there was the aggressive approach 'give me some money or else'. One day he brought a blunt knife on one of these aggressive visits, as usual I was in my room alone when he barged in. To be fair to him I don't think he had any intention of using it, but he did threaten me and it took a little while to talk him down. Indeed I took the knife off him and kept it for many years as a souvenir.

Things were going from bad to worse, colleagues were complaining about the frequency of his visits and causing upset in the waiting room. I could not breach him for failing to keep appointments, quite the contrary; I could hardly keep him away. However, one day he came in an aggressive mood and I refused his request for any money. I took him to the door to eject him and as he walked away from me, cursing over his shoulder, he picked up a stray brick and threw it through the window of the adjacent building. Given that there was only one window in the side of that building looking out onto our narrow alleyway, I would have been hard pressed to lob a brick through that single first floor window. He in his drunken state, however, did it with aplomb. The building owners complained, Billy was arrested and I laid Information for breach of the order, based upon his failure to be of good behaviour, which was part of the order in those days.

During this spell he had lost his home. I reported to the court all that had been done and said that I felt that he was no longer responding to probation and that they should now sentence him again for his original offence. I did not propose any alternative, but the court decided to make him subject of a suspended sentence in respect of the original offence. It was not long before, after another minor theft he was on his way to the local prison for a few weeks.

I will not detail all that happened thereafter, it's taken this long to give you the flavour of the first six months of the 11 years, and I will run out of paper if I go on at that level of description. So let me try to summarise some of the happenings. I found him various flats over the years and by the end he was *persona non grata* in all the places and with all the landlords I knew about. When he next appeared for a minor crime, I suggested he be seen by the local psychiatrist who dealt with the drunks of the day. He was offered voluntary treatment as part of another probation order, which of course didn't last very long. Then he went on to live rough or stay with other alcoholics, who had, usually only temporarily, found their own accommodation. He kept appearing in court for drunkenness. In the winter when I knew he was sleeping rough, that he wasn't paying his fines for the frequent appearances for drunkenness and I felt that he needed some respite, I waited till the weather got really cold and then I reminded the warrant office that he was in arrears and that he was normally in town every day. So we got him picked up taken to the local prison for seven or fourteen days for fine default, but at least it got him three square meals a day and a bit of warmth and a roof over his head.

On a later occasion, I made another try with a probation order because he had started to show some signs that he might be susceptible to help again. I found him a place in a hostel again, subject to an order. It didn't last very long. I remember a lovely telephone message Eric had left for me, "Guess who's broken all the windows in the hostel and told the warden to stick his help up his arse and is on his way down to see you."

A slight digression is needed to say a little more about Eric, so that you can understand why it was he that accompanied me to the funeral. He had been invalided out of his former very physical job in public service. He was late fifties and wanted to work. He became our receptionist. He and I got on very well and he had a lot of sympathy for my clients who suffered from capacity or mental illness problems. He had served in the Second World War and I understood his sense of humour. He was much loved by all the office typists and was very kind to them but with a wry sense of fun.

He held court at reception, a low three foot six inch high counter with no security screen, and would talk to the clients like Billy whilst they were waiting. Again his sense of humour would not be tolerated today. At one time I had three clients who it seemed, were always in the office. Billy, Stephen, of the broken toilet, and David of the Shed / wardrobe and all had significant capacity/illness issues. There was at the time a children's series called the 'Bumblies', created by Michael Bentine and involving some charming but inept characters from outer space. Eric christened Billy, Stephen and David Bumbly Numbers 1, 2 & 3. When one of them came Eric would announce to me on the telephone Bumbly Number whatever to see you. Definitely completely "un-PC", but done with love.

Billy was well known to the local police. They took him for what he was, a sad case of limited capacity and unlike many homeless drunks they dealt with he was rarely aggressive. Many had a soft spot for him. His simple friendly personality was known to police officers in other neighbouring areas, and many is the time that he wandered off to another nearby town and instead of arresting him for drunkenness, with all the paperwork involved, they would drive him to our City boundary and tell him to keep walking into town.

I suppose looking back, for all the tough times I gave him, I was still a significant person in his life. He would come to the office, increasingly over the years in a drunken state, he would talk to Eric if I was out, and if I was in I would spend a bit of time with him and try to be encouraging, but I knew that his addiction and his own capacity were total bars to his being 'cured', and that sadly life was a downward spiral. Very often I knew that the state he was in would render him liable to arrest for drunkenness, and so I would arrange for him to sleep on one of the office benches, or even, if I was report writing, in my office on the floor, just to ensure that he wasn't being awkward to members of the public or wasting police time. I wanted to do more for him, I cared for him, but I was unable to help him except at a few points in his life.

As with other city alcoholics, they visit ministers of religion to plead their, usually dire, circumstances. Father Parker at a large city centre Catholic Church was one of his favourites. He got no money, but, in the winter a sandwich and a cup of tea in front of the fire were welcome.

Periods of attempting to reform did happen, and the last one involved in him becoming involved with a vicar and some of the parishioners of the church where his funeral later took place. That church, like me initially, had tried to help. And, as with me, for a while things had gone fine, until the demon drink took hold again for what became the final time. He had almost made it through the cold nights; spring was nearly upon us when he went to a derelict house, where, together with other alcoholics, he was dossing down at night. The circumstances of his tragic death were reported in our local newspaper. It would appear that one of the other drunks lit a fire which got out of control before anybody noticed. Sadly, the fire was downstairs and Billy was sleeping upstairs, and before he became aware of the danger, the downstairs was already ablaze, preventing his escape. The paper talks graphically of the fire brigade arriving to see and hear a man calling for help from an upstairs window, claiming that he could not jump because his foot had become trapped in a toilet. Before they could effect a rescue he was badly burned, and despite being transferred to a specialist burns unit in another city he died the following day.

It was particularly poignant to Eric, who had been retired early through injury from his previous occupation in the local Fire Brigade.

In the church were gathered about half a dozen parishioners who had recently, and for a few months previously, been involved with Billy, in, what had turned out to be, the vain hope that they could reform him. Then there was Eric and I. The coffin came in and was wheeled on a trolley to the front of the church, where the vicar began the funeral service. Shortly after he had started, the back doors burst open, and in weaved a drunken man who staggered to the front of the church and threw onto the top of the coffin a bunch of flowers...................... pretty, yellow daffodils, no doubt courtesy of the Council Parks Department. He collapsed sobbing on the floor. The vicar, to his great credit, carried on.

It was a sad end to a life of ducking and diving. It was a tragic way to go. But it was, I suggest, the fate of many of the city centre drunks of that era, to not live out full lives.

I like to believe that he would have counted me as one of his many friends; and that is how I saw him.

R.I.P. Billy

Appendix 2

Slips of the report writer's pen

In chapter twelve, I made reference to my colleague Mike, and his most wonderful, tongue in cheek, insertion into a social enquiry report about the former deep sea diver. That example, together with the less good one I gave from my own work, suggests that the only 'funnies' in reports were those that we intended to be there. Well of course, like any other report writing, mistakes can be made, due to being in haste, seeing things only in one context and not realising they might have other meanings when read out of context, or poor proofreading, and they therefore may not be corrected before 'publication'. Over the years I collected a number of these and it seems appropriate to reveal some of them in this appendix.

I should perhaps explain that whilst most were derived from social enquiry reports in criminal cases, there are two other categories of report writing that I have drawn upon in collating what follows. Firstly, a small number of reports from social workers, and secondly a few more examples of mistakes made by trainee police officers. For a short period, I was appointed as a part-time lecturer, at a university which had a Department of Police Studies. In this department, trainee police officers were confronted with lectures and information about human behaviour, on the basis that they could take this into account in later years when dealing with people. Much of my work was in assessing essays, which formed the basis of assessment of their passing, or failing the course; and for those passing, grading their efforts. There are also a couple of apocryphal "slips".

Let's start with:-

My juvenile court reports were never as interesting as this.
"In the preparation of this report have had two interviews with Billy in my office and I have visited his home where I had several sessions with his mother."

Career change needed?
"This man suffers from moral unemployment. He trained as a butcher, but subsequently turned vegetarian."

Unusual death, or part a mixture of the Latvian Capital and part of a door lock?
"....Riga Mortice had begun to set in." Rigor mortis?

That's the young for you!
"This young man divides his time between servicing his motorbike and his girlfriend."
"He had an on, off, relationship with his girlfriend"

Stating the obvious?
"Shoplifting is a name given to theft that occurs in shops".
"A sudden death is where somebody suddenly dies"

We have not got the resources
"Whilst being aware that prostitution is a problem locally, I must to inform the court that we have no officers trained in this work."

Naughty, naughty, you little devil.
"The offence was more serious because it was rascally motivated" Racially?

The disadvantages of not having local justice?
"The defendant was found guilty after a trail". We do mean trial, I think.

Use of an Ouija Board?
"I liaised with the deceased daughter" I think we mean the deceased's

129

Even grander Larceny?
"The defendant has pleaded guilty to swelling house burglary".

Candidate for promotion to CID?
"Due to the circumstances that the suspect had no documentation on her, and had come into the country using a passport that was not her own, gave me the suspicion that she was an illegal immigrant"

Nearly got it right
"The defendant has been seen a psychiatrist, who reports no sign of mental health". Illness?

"At 54 years of age his present offence will be viewed as very serious, especially as he has five previous convictions for Drinking Whilst Disqualified". Driving?

"And I would ask the court to add the condition to the Order that Smith undergoes 20 sessions of Insensitive Supervision." Intensive?

"This premeditated our actions" Predetermined perhaps?

"The suspect suffered from asparagus syndrome...." Asperger's perhaps?

Unhelpful missing letters
He only meant to scare the complainant, came out as *"he only meant to scar the complainant"* – quite a difference in the court assessing seriousness and culpability.

Smith's objective to avoiding offending, came out as *"Smith's objection to avoiding offending"*- That's a naughty boy then.

Been laying concrete?
"The wife came down to find the husband lying in the kitchen floor" On?

Mixed metaphors or auto-suggestiveness?
"The events leading up to the offence of arson started when he attended a house warming party."

Man employed as a jockey. *"He had a stable upbringing"*

Father a train driver. *"Clearly the son has gone off the rails".*

Man commits an offence of assault at a funeral.
"His violent actions give rise to grave concern."

Man with vision impairment on one side due to industrial accident. Part of the supervision plan was to get him into work
"I have asked him to go regularly to the Job centre to keep an eye out for vacancies."

"He worked in a Banana factory."   What? Straightening them?

Solicitor representing man charged with indecent assault on female
"My client admits the matter; indeed even at the police station he made a clean breast of things."

"I have had access to the persecution documents."
Unlikely; prosecution documents more likely. Much the same either way I guess.

"The cutlery was smashed on the floor"   Unlikely! The crockery may have been.

"John has consistently expressed an interest in becoming a motor mechanic. Consequently I have got him a job at the local butchers."

And Finally,
"Dealing with Mrs Smith is very difficult, as she is doubly incontinent, and it all falls on the shoulders of one carer"

Printed in Great Britain
by Amazon